THE BIBLE AS LITERATURE:
THE NEW TESTAMENT

About the Author

Buckner B. Trawick is Professor of English at the University of Alabama. He received his B.A. degree from Emory University and his M.A. and Ph.D. degrees from Harvard University, where he has participated in additional research on a Ford Foundation Fellowship. Prior to his present position, Dr. Trawick held teaching positions at Clemson College, the University of Mississippi, and Temple University. He is the author also of *World Literature* (2 vols.) and of *The Bible as Literature: The Old Testament and the Apocrypha* in the Barnes & Noble Outline Series.

THE BIBLE
AS LITERATURE
THE NEW TESTAMENT

BUCKNER B. TRAWICK, *Professor of English*
University of Alabama

BARNES & NOBLE BOOKS
A DIVISION OF HARPER & ROW, PUBLISHERS
New York, Hagerstown, San Francisco, London

L.C. Catalogue Card Number: 64–22589

ISBN: 0-06-460057-2

88 89 90   20 19 18 17 16 15 14

Manufactured in the United States of America

Preface

The Bible is one of the most fascinating books ever written, and sometimes one of the most puzzling. This Outline is an attempt to catch and to share with others some of its fascination and to help solve some of its puzzling passages. It is hoped that the book will prove useful to the average lay reader, as well as to the student primarily interested in the Scriptures as literature.

This volume deals with the books of the New Testament—the Gospels, the Acts of the Apostles, the Epistles, and the Book of Revelation. Although the principal emphasis is on *literary* rather than religious or ethical qualities, any significant discussion of Biblical literature necessarily deals with content as well as technique; and it must offer interpretations of some of the content. A determined effort has been made to bring to the reader a compendium of the most up-to-date scholarship on the Bible which will be of value and interest to Protestant, Catholic, Jew, or skeptic; several points of view are presented on controversial matters.

In the belief that the King James Bible is still the best *literary* version, that has been chosen as the basis for this book. It is hoped, however, that readers who prefer the Douay, the Revised Standard, the New English, or the Jewish version will find the Outline equally helpful.

The Bible as Literature: The New Testament is supplemented by a companion Outline, *The Bible as Literature: The Old Testament and the Apocrypha* (2nd ed.; Barnes & Noble, 1970), which discusses in similar fashion every book of the Old Testament and the Apocrypha. Thus together the two volumes offer the reader a commentary on all eighty books of the King James Bible.

B.B.T.

Acknowledgments

The author received much assistance in the preparation of this volume from the numerous sources cited in the Notes on pp. 153–162. The chart on p. 3, as well as many facts, dates, and discussions, were based upon *The Interpreter's Bible* (12 vols.) published by the Abingdon Press, Nashville, Tenn., 1951–1957.

Table of Contents

THE BIBLE AS LITERATURE:
THE NEW TESTAMENT

1

Backgrounds of the New Testament

Nearly all our information concerning the life and teachings of Jesus and the activities of his followers during the first Christian century is derived from the twenty-seven books that comprise the New Testament: the four "Gospels"; an account of the activities of Paul and other leaders of the Church; twenty-one epistles; and an apocalypse.

The word *testament* is the English translation of the Greek *diatheke*, which means "covenant." In fact, "New Covenant" would be a more accurate title for the last twenty-seven books of the Bible. The "Old Covenant" between God and the Jewish people—the agreement made with Abraham and reconfirmed with Moses, the promise by God to prosper the nation if it would worship him and obey his commandments—this "Old Covenant" is now superseded (for Christians) by a "New Covenant": God promises to reward with eternal life in the Kingdom of Heaven every man who accepts Christ, loves God with all his strength and mind and soul, and loves his neighbor as himself. Thus in the New Testament individual rather than national righteousness is stressed, and the emphasis is shifted from material rewards in the present to spiritual rewards in the afterlife. The New Testament, then, proclaims a new relationship between God and man.

There are several obvious differences between the literature of the Old Testament and that of the New. In the first place, whereas the Old Testament is a collection of national literature, containing many different literary types and reflecting an evolving national culture, the New Testament is a strictly sectarian volume made up of the writings of a small group of the followers of Jesus. In the second place, the composition of the Old Testament covered a period of perhaps a thousand years, but all of the New Testament was written, it is believed, within the seventy-five-year

1

period from A.D. 50 to 125. (Some authorities prefer a hundred-year-period, A.D. 51–150.) Finally, in the New Testament there is a very different "spiritual climate" [1] from that in the Old; the early Christians were convinced that the long-awaited Messiah had come, and therefore their writings are full of joy, hope, and the urgency to spread the gospel (or "good news") of Jesus' message.

HISTORICAL BACKGROUND

The historical background of the New Testament begins two centuries after the Maccabean rebellion, and the New Testament books reflect changed political, social, and cultural conditions in Palestine. The Hasmonaean (Maccabean) dynasty had continued to rule the Jewish people for several decades. In 67 B.C. John Hyrcanus II (the grandson of John Hyrcanus I) had been defeated in battle by his brother Aristobulus II, who had made himself both king and high priest. After trying unsuccessfully to regain his throne, John Hyrcanus had appealed to Rome for help. In response, Pompey the Great had marched into Palestine in 63 B.C., wiped out the forces of Aristobulus, and placed John Hyrcanus over the Jewish state, but with the title of "ethnarch" (provincial governor) instead of "king." In 40 B.C. Octavius Caesar had made Herod the Great * "king of Judea" (in effect, king of all Palestine), thus putting an end to the Hasmonaean line.

Herod ruled with a firm hand. He was hated by the Jews for his subservience to Rome, his sponsoring of Greek and Roman customs, his extortion of high taxes, and his cruelty toward all he suspected of being his enemies. To him Matthew (Ch. 2) attributes the "slaughter of the innocents" at the time of Jesus' birth.

Upon Herod's death in 4 B.C.† his kingdom was divided among

---

[1] For all notes indicated by raised numbers, see pp. 111 ff.

* The name "Herod" is likely to become confusing to readers of the New Testament, for it is used to refer to four different rulers: (1) Herod the Great, king of Judea, 40-4 B.C.; (2) Herod Antipas (son of Herod the Great), tetrarch of Galilee, 4 B.C.–A.D. 39; (3) Herod Agrippa I (grandson of Herod the Great), ruler of all three sections of Palestine at various times between A.D. 37 and 44 (see chart); and (4) Herod Agrippa II (son of Herod Agrippa I), ruler of part of Iturea, A.D. 53-93, and of Galilee, ca. A.D. 54-93.

† For a discussion of the discrepancies in Matthew's dates of the birth of Jesus and the death of Herod the Great, see note ‡, p. 56 below.

Chart of Roman and Palestinian Events During New Testament Times [*]

Rome	Palestine			New Testament
First Triumvirate: Julius Caesar, Pompey, Crassus, 60 B.C.	Conquest of Jerusalem by Pompey, 63 B.C. John Hyrcanus II, 63–40 B.C.			
Second Triumvirate; Octavius, Lepidus, Antony, 43 B.C.				
Augustus (Octavius), 31 B.C.–A.D. 14	Herod the Great, nominated 40 B.C., reigned 37–4 B.C.			Jesus born before spring of 4 B.C.
	Iturea, Trachonitis, Etc.	Galilee	Judea	
	Philip, 4 B.C.–A.D. 34	Herod Antipas, 4 B.C.–A.D. 39	Archelaus, 4 B.C.–A.D. 6 Procurators, A.D. 6–41 (Pilate, A.D. 26–36)	Baptism of Jesus, ca. A.D. 28 Crucifixion, ca. A.D. 31. Conversion of Paul, ca. A.D. 32
Tiberius, A.D. 14–37	Agrippa I, A.D. 37–44	Agrippa I, A.D. 39–44		
Caligula, A.D. 37–41 Claudius, A.D. 41–54			Agrippa I, A.D. 41–44	
Nero, A.D. 54–68	Agrippa II, A.D. 53–93	Agrippa II, A.D. 54–93	Procurators, A.D. 44–66 (Felix, A.D. 52–60; Festus, A.D. 61–62)	Paul before Festus, ca. A.D. 61 Paul in Rome, ca. A.D. 62
Galba, Otho, Vitellius, A.D. 68		First revolt of the Jews, A.D. 66		
Vespasian, A.D. 69–79		Jerusalem falls to Titus, A.D. 70		

* For most of this chart, the author is indebted to the chart by Georges A. Barrois, in "Chronology, Metrology, Etc.," *IB*, I, 150. The dates pertaining to Paul are in some cases different from those given below, p. 82.

3

three of his sons: (1) Philip (referred to in Luke 3:1,19) received the northeast portion around Mount Hermon, which he ruled till his death in A.D. 34; he was given the title of "tetrarch" (ruler over a fourth of a province). (2) Herod Antipas (mentioned frequently in the Gospels) ruled as the tetrarch of Galilee and Perea till A.D. 39, when he was removed and banished to Gaul. (3) Archelaus was made ethnarch of the region which included Judea, Samaria, and Idumea. By A.D. 6 the rule of Archelaus had become so oppressive that the Jews and the Samaritans appealed to Rome for relief. Archelaus was removed, and Judea became an imperial province, governed by procurators directly responsible to the emperor himself; this form of government continued till A.D. 41. (It was Pontius Pilate, procurator from A.D. 26 to 36, who condemned Jesus to be crucified.)

After the death of Philip in A.D. 34, the northeast territory was attached to the province of Syria. Three years later Caligula succeeded Tiberius as emperor and made Agrippa (Herod Agrippa I) king of the former tetrarchy of Philip. When Herod Antipas was banished in A.D. 39, his domain was made part of Agrippa's kingdom. Upon the accession of Claudius in A.D. 41, the province of Judea (including Samaria and Idumea) was taken from under the procurators and also made a part of Agrippa's kingdom. Thus Agrippa I, grandson of the Hasmonaean princess Mariamne and so partially Jewish, ruled over a united Palestine. Unfortunately, his beneficent and popular reign was short. He died in A.D. 44, and Judea was once more placed under a procurator.

During the lifetime of Jesus the Jews in Palestine were allowed a considerable degree of self-government. The Romans granted broad executive, legislative, and judicial powers to the Great Sanhedrin of Jerusalem, a council composed of seventy-one Jewish elders (most of them Sadducees, some Pharisees). (See pp. 5, 26.) The presiding officer of the council was the high priest. The Sanhedrin was permitted to enforce the Jewish laws but could not impose the death penalty. Taxes to be paid to Rome were collected by "publicans," local Jews hated by the people not only because they were minions of Rome but also because they had won a reputation as extortioners. The privilege of becoming a publican went to the highest bidder, who was allowed to keep all the taxes he could collect over and above what he paid for his position.

It should be emphasized that during the lifetime of Jesus and throughout the period of the first-century emperors, Romans were interested chiefly in public order, submission to them, and material wealth, not in a spiritual life or a higher religion. In Roman religion the gods were animistic powers governing the everyday world. The emperor Octavius and his successors were considered divine, and all outsiders were to be obedient subjects. The teachings of Jesus and the work of the Disciples (always stressing the worth, faith, and unique personality of the individual) represented the antithesis of Rome's materialistic, efficient, comfortable system of law and order. The various Jewish groups with their moral standards and religious faith were tolerated—provided that the *system* was not thereby greatly disturbed or endangered. Many in these groups feared that the individualistic morality of Jesus would offend the Romans and bring repression to the entire community. The Romans made no attempt to settle the political or religious disputes among the Jewish groups of Palestine, nor did they at first care much about the new religion which took a stand on basic questions, ignoring disputes about the trivial details of religious customs. Much time was to elapse before the Romans became alert to the fact that the new teachings of the early Christians did not mean retirement from the practical world of affairs but rather introduced an intellectual anarchism (from their point of view), endangering established institutions and corrupt practices so rife in high places.

The four main socio-political groups of Palestine which influenced the thinking and teaching of Jesus were as follows: (1) The *Sadducees* were a small but powerful group of conservative aristocrats, from whose ranks the hereditary priesthood was drawn. In matters of doctrine they accepted only the written Law of Moses, rejecting the oral tradition and interpretation cherished by their opponents, the Pharisees. The Sadducees did not believe in the resurrection of the dead, the existence of angels and demons, or the approaching advent of a Messiah to save the Israelites from their oppressors. The Pharisees condemned the Sadducees for collaboration with Rome.[2] (2) The *Pharisees* were the large group of rabbis or interpreters of the Hebraic Law. Not only did they emphasize strict observance of the Law, but also they felt that a continuous reinterpretation of that Law was necessary in order to keep it currently applicable to daily life.

The Pharisees were violently opposed to the adoption of Greek and Roman customs. (3) The *Herodians* were eager partisans of the Herod dynasty. (4) The *Zealots* were a party of ardent patriots who strove and plotted to throw off Roman rule. They regarded the Sadducees as "collaborators" with Rome, and they believed the Pharisees too pacifistic. During the first century A.D. they instigated and led many revolts, including the rebellion which brought on Titus' destruction of Jerusalem in A.D. 70. Although the word *Zealot* rarely occurs in the New Testament, it is thought that various figures, such as Barabbas, Judas Iscariot, and many who expected Jesus to lead a political rebellion, belonged to this radical party.

In addition to the foregoing, a quite different group were the *Essenes*. Though not mentioned in the New Testament, they are believed to have influenced the teachings of John the Baptist, the early education of Jesus, and the theology of the Gospel of John. The Essenes were an extremely pious sect of only a few thousand men who emphasized celibacy and simplicity of life. They formed a communal fraternity and virtually isolated themselves from the rest of mankind. (There were several groups of the Essenes; some did marry as a means of continuing the community, whereas others adopted children and welcomed worthy immigrants from outside.) The Essenes were fervent believers in the imminent appearance of the long-expected Messiah. It has been suggested that the ablutions which were part of their rituals of bodily purification were the source of the Christian practice of baptism.[3] Some scholars believe that it was a community of Essenes who copied and preserved the famous Dead Sea Scrolls discovered in the fifth and sixth decades of the twentieth century. (See discussion of the Dead Sea Scrolls, p. 97.)

NEW TESTAMENT HISTORY AND BIOGRAPHY

The historico-biographical literature of the New Testament differs from that of the Old Testament and Maccabean periods in purpose, method, and language. It is difficult to assign a literary classification to the first five books of the New Testament. Students of literature, however, may conveniently consider the Gospels and Acts as a part of Biblical history and biography. Whatever the authors' several purposes, all five books are historical in their depiction of the founding of the Christian Church at a time when Palestine was under Roman jurisdiction, and all are biographical in depicting some events in the lives of Jesus and his early followers. But none was formally intended as an impartial history or a complete biography, and all incidentally encompass various literary types, such as fiction (parables), oratory, and theological debate.

The difficulty which literary historians have found in trying to classify these five books obviously lies in the fact that each is a special sort of biography or history—special because it is propagandistic.* The authors wrote not to record some interesting facts about a man and an era, but to spread the "good news" (the meaning of the word *Gospel*) about God's relationship to man, good news which would completely transform the lives of all who read (or heard) and believed. An integral part of the good news was the revolutionary code of ethics taught by Jesus; and hence the authors, as each saw fit, included sermons, anecdotes, and moral precepts. The propagandistic purpose of the books also explains the omission of material which one might expect in a historico-biographical narrative. There was simply no need, for instance, to record the events of Jesus' childhood and youth; for the Evangelists that portion of his life had little or no bearing on the message which he—and they—wanted to tell to all the world. Other omissions and inclusions depended upon the specific audiences to which the various authors addressed their writings.

Many critics have considered the Gospels, Acts, and some of the epistles of the New Testament inferior as literature to most of the books of the Old Testament. C. A. Dinsmore, however, maintains that the Gospels, especially, are excellent pieces of writing:

The evangelists may not have been men of trained artistic abilities. They could not weave sentences as delicate silk into exquisite patterns, but they did possess the cardinal virtues of effective writing—sincerity and simplicity. . . . It is because the evangelists were so sincere and unambitious to obtrude themselves that they let the splendor of their Lord shine through their very weaknesses. They accomplished their purpose: the great Figure stands forth in its essential glory.[4]

---

* The word *propagandistic* is not used here in a derogatory sense. *Propaganda* originally meant "things which must be spread abroad."

Although there is much divergence of opinion concerning the historical accuracy of the Gospels and Acts, even modernist scholars are willing to accept as reliable a large proportion of the accounts given in these books. Certain facts, however, should be acknowledged.

In the first place, we must be aware that both the words of Jesus and the accounts of his deeds were preserved for several decades only by oral transmission. Like Socrates, Jesus (though well educated) wrote nothing; at least, we have no report that he ever wrote anything except the few words he wrote in the sand with his finger (John 8:6). Since there was no stenographer to record his sayings verbatim, our knowledge of what he said is derived entirely from what his followers remembered. (Life was then short, and perhaps only a few of them survived until the first of the writings.) There was a lapse of forty years or more (most scholars believe) between the Crucifixion and the composition of the earliest Gospel. The probable reason for this gap is that the original Christians felt no need for written records of the Master's life and sayings, because they anticipated his imminent Second Coming. During the course of forty years, men's memories become blurred and cannot be expected to retain details with perfect accuracy.

Furthermore, there is the obstacle of language. It is almost certain that Jesus spoke and taught in Aramaic, the everyday language of the Galilean peasant. But our Gospels are in Greek. Whether it was the Evangelists themselves or some intermediaries who first told the Gospel stories in Greek, there was at some stage the danger of inaccurately translating the Aramaic words of Jesus. True, there is an ancient tradition, transmitted from the second century A.D., that the Gospel according to Matthew was written first in Aramaic. Several modern scholars have concluded that all four Gospels and the book of Acts were written in Aramaic; grammatical constructions and idioms in these books indicate an underlying Aramaic version. No such versions, however, have been discovered, and it is therefore customary for Biblical scholars to treat the Greek text of the Gospels and Acts as if it were the "original." The various epistles and the book of Revelation were almost certainly written first in Greek.

COMPOSITION, COLLECTION, AND CANONIZATION

The opening verses of Luke imply the existence of numerous Gospels during the first century A.D., among which are included our surviving four canonized books. These surviving ones were not written as a co-operative project, but were composed for different groups in different parts of the world. The authorship of all but Luke (and its sequel, Acts) is disputed.

All the canonical books of the New Testament were probably written during a period of five decades—most of them during the four decades A.D. 64 to 105 (the death of Jesus may be dated about A.D. 32). There is virtually no clue to when or how these books were first collected. Apparently what happened is that the various Christian communities treasured highly the writings of the Apostles and the early missionaries; copied them innumerable times; and distributed the copies among other churches. Obviously, these writings, along with the Old Testament, were zealously protected from the numerous forces of destruction which threatened them, and the writings were handed down from generation to generation; but the details of preservation and transmission are unknown.

In addition to the twenty-seven books which for about sixteen centuries have always been included in the New Testament canon, there were many other writings in the infancy of Christianity which were considered more or less sacred by certain individuals and by certain churches. The prologue to Luke (1:1), for example, indicates the very early existence of several other biographies of Jesus; at least twenty-six other Gospels are known to have existed by the end of the fifth century. Many Christian writings other than Gospels were circulated. The principal problem of canonization, then, seems to have been at first one of exclusion. As time passed, certain books were condemned either on the basis of the harmful or heretical nature of their doctrines or on the basis of the lateness of their composition. For several centuries after the death of Jesus, there was no central church organization nor any individual who exercised enough authority to persuade the far-flung churches to accept as sacred any particular group of writings. In 367 Athanasius, Bishop of Alexandria, suggested in a letter that the twenty-seven books in our present New Testament be accepted as the canon. In 382 the Synod of Rome, influenced by St. Jerome, adopted officially the list offered by Athanasius; this adoption was later affirmed by the churches in North Africa and eastern Europe.

The order of the books was partially established by the Vulgate, but it was St. Augustine (in his *Concerning Doctrine* ii, 8, written *ca.* 397) who gave us the exact order now followed.

GREEK AND LATIN VERSIONS

There are several thousand known manuscripts of the Greek New Testament. The most important are the codices Vaticanus, Sinaiticus, Alexandrinus, and Ephraemi.

The Latin-speaking Christians certainly possessed translations from the Greek Scriptures as early as the second century—probably during the first. About fifty Old Latin manuscripts of the New Testament still survive; the earliest are from the fourth or fifth century. In addition to these texts, so many quotations appear in the writings of the Latin church fathers, such as Tertullian, St. Jerome, St. Augustine, and Pelagius, that it is believed that virtually the whole of the New Testament could be reproduced from them in Old Latin.

The Vulgate version of the New Testament is a revision of the then-current Old Latin version; St. Jerome used the Greek text as the basis for his emendations. Although the Old Latin and the Vulgate versions of the New Testament were both used for centuries, the superiority of St. Jerome's revision (as was the case with the Old Testament) eventually led to its adoption by Christian readers. The Vulgate New Testament contained the twenty-seven books now accepted as canonical.*

SIMILARITIES IN THE FOUR GOSPELS

In view of the difficulties of transmission, it is remarkable that the four accounts of the ministry of Jesus have so much in common and that the picture we get of Jesus in each is so consistent with that given in the others.

All four Gospels tell about John the Baptist's ministry, Jesus' healing of the son of the centurion, the controversies between

* For a summary of the history of the English Bible, see *The Bible as Literature: The Old Testament and the Apocrypha* (2nd ed.; New York: Barnes and Noble, Inc., 1970), a companion Outline by the present author.

Jesus and his enemies, the feeding of the five thousand, Jesus' walking on the water, the woman's anointing of Jesus, the cleansing of the Temple, the triumphal entry into Jerusalem, and the Resurrection.[5] All depict a peripatetic Master who confronts his twelve Disciples, other individuals, and sometimes multitudes of people with miracles, statements of doctrine, debates, public controversies, sermons, and parables or allegories.

Jesus found especially effective as a pedagogical device the *parable*, a homespun analogy used (1) sometimes to illustrate a principle concretely, in terms of Palestinian daily life (a story about a mustard seed, a lost sheep, a sower, or a bottle of wine) and (2) sometimes to make the listener deduce a truth for himself ("Which now of these three, thinkest thou, was neighbor unto him that fell among the thieves?"—Luke 10:36). Note that Mark, Matthew, and Luke (or later revisers) seem occasionally to have mistaken Jesus' purpose and to have considered parables a means of concealing the truth instead of a means of clarifying it (see Mark 4:10-12; Matt. 13:10-15; and Luke 8:9-10). Some of the parables appear to have been altered by later revisionists.[6] On occasion there may have been confusion between a parable and a miracle or other deed of Jesus (for example, the parable of the fruitless fig tree in Luke 13:6-9 and the miracle of Jesus' cursing of the fruitless fig tree in Mark 11:12-14, 20–21).

Together Mark, Matthew, and Luke record about forty-one parables, as listed in the accompanying table. According to many commentators the Gospel of John contains no parables, but the distinction between parables and John's "allegories" of the Good Shepherd and of the Vine and the Branches (10:7-16 and 15:1-8) is a very fine one.

DIFFERENCES IN THE FOUR GOSPELS

The four Gospels and Acts are believed to have been written for four different social groups. They present the life and teachings of Jesus from four different points of view:

Mark—written for Gentiles of Rome to demonstrate that Jesus was the Messiah and to encourage Christians suffering from Roman persecution.

Matthew—written for Jewish Christians and (at least partially) for Gentiles of Asia Minor, to present a fuller biography of Jesus and to record more teachings than Mark and to emphasize that Christianity was not overthrowing but fulfilling Jewish law.

Parable	Mark	Matt.	Luke
The House on the Rock and the House on the Sand		7:24–27	6:47–49
New Patches on Old Garments	2:21	9:16	5:36
New Wine in Old Wineskins	2:22	9:17	5:37–38
The Two Debtors			7:36–50
The Backsliding Demoniac		12:43–45	11:24–26
The Sower	4:3–20	13:3–23	8:4–15
The Good Samaritan			10:25–37
The Growing Seed	4:26–29		
The Importunate Friend			11:5–10
The Tares		13:36–43	
The Rich Fool			12:16–21
The Barren Fig Tree			13:6–9
The Mustard Seed	4:30–32	13:31–32	13:18–19
The Leaven		13:33	13:20–21
The Hidden Treasure		13:44	
The Pearl of Great Price		13:45–46	
The Dragnet		13:47–50	
The Impolite Wedding Guest			14:7–11
The Banquet			14:16–24
The Tower Builder			14:28–30
The King Preparing for War			14:31–33
The Lost Sheep		18:12–14	15:3–7
The Unmerciful Servant		18:23–35	
The Lost Coin			15:8–10
The Laborers in the Vineyard		20:1–16	
The Prodigal Son			15:11–32
The Dishonest Steward			16:1–9
The Rich Man and Lazarus			16:19–31
The Farmer and His Servant			17:7–10
The Persistent Widow and the Unjust Judge			18:1–8
The Pharisee and the Publican			18:9–14
The Two Sons		21:28–32	
The Wicked Husbandmen	12:1–12	21:33–48	20:9–19
The Wedding Feast		22:1–14	
The Budding Fig Tree	13:28–29	24:32–33	21:29–31
The Watchful Servants	13:34–37		12:35–38
The Householder and the Thief		24:42–44	12:36–40
The Wise Steward		24:45–51	12:42–48
The Ten Virgins		25:1–13	
The Talents (or Pounds)		25:14–30	19:11–27
The Sheep and the Goats		25:31–46	

Luke—Acts—addressed to a Roman official and written perhaps to convince the imperial government that the Christians were not a subversive sect.

John—addressed to a more theological-minded and philosophical group than the other Gospels. John's chronological position is uncertain: once thought to reflect Greek mysticism, the Gospel of John is now believed by some commentators to reflect a more purely Hebraic tradition.

THE SYNOPTIC PROBLEM

The five books which stand at the beginning of the New Testament fall into three separate groups: (1) the so-called "Synoptic" Gospels—Mark, Matthew, and Luke; (2) the Gospel of John; and (3) the Acts of the Apostles. The Gospel of Luke and the book of Acts are believed to have been written by the same author and, indeed, to have been originally a single document.

It has long been recognized that the Gospels according to Mark, Matthew, and Luke bear a striking resemblance to one another in contents and arrangement. Because their contents may readily be placed in a "harmony" [7] made up of parallel columns, these books have been called *synoptic,* that is, "affording or taking a common view."

Which of these books was written first? Which came second? Which borrowed from the other (or others)? These questions— involving attempts to establish the relationship of each book to the others—are known as the "Synoptic Problem." [8] After much intensive study of such matters as diction, order of events, and repetition, the majority of Biblical scholars today agree on the following conclusions: (1) Mark was written earliest of the three, and Matthew and Luke borrowed much of their narrative contents from Mark. At least 610 of Mark's 661 verses are paralleled in either Matthew or Luke.[9] (2) Both Matthew and Luke used another Greek document, designated "Q" (from the German *Quelle,* meaning "source"), made up chiefly of the sayings of Jesus. (3) There were further sources no longer extant from which Matthew and Luke drew material. In brief, there is wide agreement that Matthew and Luke were written at about the same time (in the latter part of the first century) but independently, though drawing much of their material from Mark, document Q, and probably other identical sources.

THE EPISTLES

The letter was a significant form of ancient religious literature. In the Bible it is not confined to the New Testament; two letters appear in the Old Testament, forming parts of the books of Ezra and Daniel, and two are in the Apocryphal II Maccabees. Many other letters of great antiquity have been preserved, written by such venerable church fathers as Barnabas; Clement, bishop of Rome; and Polycarp, bishop of Smyrna. Some of these were considered for inclusion in the New Testament canon, along with the twenty-seven books which have been traditionally accepted.

Of inestimable historical and doctrinal value as the oldest extant Christian writings,* some of the epistles—especially those of Paul and John—have, in addition, great literary merit.

All the New Testament letters were probably written between A.D. 50 and 150. Most of them are rather formal, "open" letters addressed to church groups; a few are addressed to individuals and hence are more personal and informal. For centuries Paul was believed to be the author of fourteen epistles; now most scholars ascribe only ten to him. Three are assigned to John, two to Peter, one to Jude, and one to James; but the authorship of all of these is a matter of dispute.

---

* Some parts of the Gospels probably antedate the epistles, but these bits were in all likelihood transmitted orally until after A.D. 70.

2

The Gospel According to Mark:
The Earliest of the Synoptics

In our New Testament, the Gospel of Mark (the forty-first book of the Bible) follows that of Matthew—probably because St. Augustine and other early commentators considered it not as a source, but as an abridgment, of Matthew. (Mark has 16 chapters, Matthew 28.) Since virtually all modern scholars believe that Mark is the oldest of the four Gospels, it will here be discussed first.

AUTHORSHIP, SOURCES, DATE, LANGUAGE

Literary historians who try to discover the origins of Mark's Gospel are concerned with problems of authorship, sources, place and date of composition, and language.

A tradition that goes back to the second century holds that the author of the first Gospel is to be identified with John Mark (Latin surname, Marcus), a companion of Peter and also of Paul in several missionary endeavors (see, e.g., Acts 15:37, II Tim. 4:11, and I Pet. 5:13); according to this tradition, Mark obtained the bulk of his material from Peter. Some scholars, however, hold that the Gospel is anonymous and that it is based upon several sources, both oral and written.[1]

It is generally agreed that, as noted above, the Gospel according to Mark was written in Rome and probably for Gentiles in that city. Pertinent evidence includes Mark's quotation of Aramaic words (followed by a translation of them) and his many explanations of Jewish customs; since the explanations were not necessary for Jewish readers, the book must have been intended primarily for Gentiles.

There is considerable disagreement about the date of composition. Some scholars, especially among Roman Catholics, assign to Mark an early date, perhaps as early as A.D. 50. Those investigators who adhere to the "Marcan-Petrine" theory believe that the book was written (A.D. 64?-67?) after the martyrdom of Paul and Peter and certainly before A.D. 75. Some authorities contend that Chapter 13 is a reflection of the destruction of Jerusalem and that therefore the book must be dated after A.D. 70; others consider that chapter a prophecy of the fall of the Holy City and so suggest an earlier date. But perhaps the majority of scholars today accept as most likely the period A.D. 70-75.

For many centuries Biblical scholars have believed that all the Gospels were first written in Greek, C. C. Torrey [2] and some others, however, have argued that the Greek versions are translations of Aramaic originals.*

Mark has been called the Gospel of Power.[3] Its primary purpose, most commentators agree, is neither historical nor biographical, but theological—to emphasize the great power of Jesus and thereby demonstrate that he was the Messiah, the Son of God. By so doing, Mark hoped to give courage and confidence to the Christians enduring the persecutions of the Roman emperors.[4]

Mark's lack of polish (along with his failure to record many of the sayings of Jesus, plus the abrupt ending of his book) † has caused many readers, both ancient and modern, to regard his Gospel as inferior to the Gospels of Matthew and Luke. Considered from a purely literary point of view, Mark does have many shortcomings, but he also has many merits.

Admittedly, his narrative structure is so loose and episodic that the story is hardly more than a string of incidents. The chronological sequence of events is often marked only by such vague and inexact transitional expressions as "after that" and "then it came to pass." [5] Many events recorded by the other Evangelists are omitted, and there is a glaring lack of proportion; for example, almost a third of the whole Gospel is devoted to telling what happened during one week of Jesus' life—the week preceding the Crucifixion. On the other hand, critics point out that the Gospel

---

* If this theory can be proved, it may push back the generally accepted date for each Gospel about twenty or twenty-five years.

† Some historians believe that the Gospel was left incomplete or that its concluding pages have been lost.

contains a "consistent development of the story [of Jesus]" and that it has a "definite dramatic structure," proceeding "from the Baptism through the Resurrection." [6] The rapidity of the action is indicated by the fact that the word translated "straightway" (K.J.V.) or "immediately" (R.S.V.) is used forty-two times.[7]

"Mark's style is direct, brief, a little rough, yet he knows how to state most disturbing facts without comment." [8] Critics who admit that Mark's diction is colloquial and uneven hasten to praise his style as simple, direct, and colorful. He was indeed a great storyteller. Contributing to the vividness and realism of his narrative are: (1) the frequent use of direct discourse; (2) the inclusion of Aramaic words; (3) occasional shifts into the historical present tense; and (4) a wealth of descriptive details and arresting figures of speech.

The tone is one of reverence, awe, and—toward the end— personal grief over the impending tragedy of the trial and Crucifixion. Mark evinces an almost childlike joy and wonder over the performance of miracles, which are to him the most impressive evidence of Jesus' divine power. His emphasis on Jesus "as an austere man of action, a worker of miracles and the mysterious fulfillment of the Messianic mission," [9] the rapidity of movement of the narrative, and the vividness of the description—all these make the reader feel that Mark was carried away by the sad and wondrous events he records.

"Without any literary skill at all, but with sheer honesty and profound faith, Mark succeeded in writing a book of surpassing vigor, heroism, challenge, and triumph." [10]

CONTENTS OF THE GOSPEL

This Gospel tells nothing whatsoever about the birth and early life of Jesus, but begins with an account of John the Baptist's proclamation of Jesus' coming and of the baptism of Jesus. Then it tells about Jesus' ministry in Galilee and in Syria and Perea, his entry into Jerusalem and his ministry there, his trial and execution, and, finally, his Resurrection and Ascension. This narrative order appears to be more "historically accurate than that in any of the other Gospels." [11] *

* This order, however, does not lend itself very readily to logical subdivision; therefore this Outline will employ some new groupings of passages, especially those concerned with Jesus' miracles and his teachings.

BAPTISM AND TEMPTATION OF JESUS (1:1-13);
THE DEATH OF JOHN THE BAPTIST (6:14-29)

After a brief announcement of his theme, Mark abruptly opens
his story with a quotation stating the ancient prophecy about one
who would come to prepare a way for the Messiah.[12] John the
Baptist, clad in a rough camel hide and a leather belt and subsist-
ing on dried locusts and wild honey, has come to fulfill this
prophecy.* Jesus comes from Nazareth, in Galilee, to a spot in
Judea, near Jerusalem and beside the river Jordan. There John
has been baptizing repentant people (especially converts to
Judaism),[13] symbolically washing away their sins. When he
baptizes Jesus, the Holy Spirit in the form of a dove descends
upon Jesus, and a voice declares: "Thou art my beloved Son,
in whom I am well pleased."

Then the Spirit sends Jesus into the wilderness, where Satan
tempts him for "forty days." Mark gives no details of the temptations described in Matthew and Luke.

It is not till Chapter 6 that Mark resumes the story of John
the Baptist. Long held a prisoner by Herod Antipas, John had
been allowed to live because Herod feared him and believed
him to be a holy man. But eventually Herodias (Herod's wife,
who had been the wife of Herod's brother and who hated John
because he had denounced her marriage to Herod) tricked her
husband into decreeing John's death. Her daughter † danced for
Herod, who was so pleased that he swore to give the girl any

---

* This picture of John is strongly reminiscent of the description of Elijah
found in I Kings 17:6 and II Kings 1:8. Some of John's audience believed him
to be a reincarnation of Elijah (Mark 6:15), and Mark seems to agree
(9:13). For Mark the great significance of John the Baptist is not his baptism
of Jesus but the fact that he was the first to recognize and proclaim Jesus'
Messiahship.

There may have been some rivalry between Jesus' followers and those of
John the Baptist; at any rate, the Gospel writers take pains to reconcile
John's mission with the Messiahship of Jesus by having John proclaim his
own inferiority (for example, Mark 1:7-8). The book of Acts (19:1-5)
relates that some converts were taken into the Christian fold who had previ-
ously known only the baptism of John the Baptist.

† The name Salome is not used by Mark or any other Biblical author, but
is supplied by secular sources.

gift she might choose, up to half his kingdom. At Herodias' instigation, the daughter asked for John's head on a charger (platter). Bound by his oath, Herod felt obliged to grant her request.*

THE CALLING OF THE DISCIPLES (1:14-20 and 3:13-19)

Returning to Galilee, Jesus begins his ministry by preaching and telling the people: "The time is fulfilled, and the kingdom of God is at hand; repent ye, and believe the gospel."

His next act is to call four Disciples (the four fishermen) to his service. He recruits his followers from the relatively humble classes, though not from the poorest or the most uneducated. They are not the lowest class of workers, but neither are they theologians, great landowners, or high officials. Jesus sees the fishermen Simon (Peter) and his brother Andrew and says to them: "Come ye after me, and I will make you to become fishers of men." Immediately they forsake their nets and follow him. James and John, who like Simon and Andrew abandon their occupation to follow Jesus, are the sons of Zebedee, a shipowner who employs laborers. Somewhat later Jesus chooses the other eight: Philip, Bartholomew, Matthew, Thomas, James (son of Alphaeus), Thaddaeus, Simon the Canaanite, and Judas Iscariot.†

---

* Mark's version of the execution contains two inaccuracies: historically, Herodias was the wife not of Philip but of another of the brothers of Herod Antipas; and Herod was not king but tetrarch of Galilee and Perea (Grant, *IB*, VII, 734).

† Jesus bids Levi, a publican (tax collector), to follow him, and Levi obeys (2:14); but Levi is not considered one of the Twelve. The Gospel of Matthew (9:9) substitutes the name "Matthew" for Levi. Luke (5:27-32) tells the story of Levi, and in another place (19:1-10) tells a similar story about Zacchaeus, which is very probably a "doublet" of the Levi narrative. All three of the Synoptic Gospels list Matthew as one of the Disciples.

Thus the names of some of the minor members of the Twelve vary a bit in the several accounts. Possibly some members were known by more than one name (for example, Matthew and Levi may have been the same person). But possibly the personnel changed while the significant number *twelve* was retained. Nathaniel and "Judas not Iscariot" may have preceded or succeeded other members in Mark's list. After the Crucifixion, Matthias was chosen to succeed Iscariot (Acts 1:26).

(Note that this Outline uses the words *Disciple* and *Apostle* interchangeably and capitalizes them when they refer to a member of the Twelve.)

METHODS OF TEACHING THE DISCIPLES AND THE PEOPLE

As has already been noted, Mark records fewer teachings of Jesus than any of the other Evangelists; it is for the account of Jesus' deeds and not mainly for his sayings that we generally read this Gospel. There are, however, many references in the book to occasions on which Jesus teaches throngs of people, and there are a few cases in which Mark cites Jesus' words as they had been reported to him. He pictures Jesus as performing miracles (or "mighty works") which convince the Disciples and the people that his power is from God. He retells and interprets various parables attributed to Jesus. He does not (as Matthew did) attempt to reproduce the text of any sermon, but he alludes to the fact that Jesus frequently addressed multitudes and taught in synagogues, and he occasionally attempts to give synopses of Jesus' doctrines. He pays a great deal of attention to controversies with Jewish socio-political parties.

MIRACLES

Mark delights in the miraculous and eagerly records each of Jesus' supernatural feats as evidence of his divine power. The Gospel records twenty specific miracles and alludes to others; these are performed at various times during Jesus' ministry. His fame spreads so rapidly that soon after the first few miracles, multitudes flock to him from all over Judea, Idumea, and Syria. Jesus seizes such opportunities to teach the people; once in order to preach, he finds it necessary to enter a boat to avoid the press of the crowds.

Most of Jesus' miracles are miracles of healing or of bringing aid or sustenance to people.*

Healing of the Ill and the Afflicted. Many times Jesus casts out demons or "unclean spirits" (1:23-26,34,39; 3:11,22; 5:1-20; 7:24-30; and 9:14-29). The authors of the Gospels—and Jesus himself—share the common belief in demons, or "unclean spirits," who take possession of people. On other occasions Jesus cures Peter's mother-in-law of a fever (1:30-31), heals a leper (1:40-45),

---

* On one occasion he curses a fig tree for failing to provide fruit for him— though it was not the season for figs; the tree withers and dies (11:12-25). Perhaps this story is a doublet of the parable of the Barren Fig Tree as told in Luke 13:6-9.

cures a paralytic (2:1-12), and restores a man's withered hand (3:1-5). In two instances he gives sight to the blind (8:22-26 and 10:46-52), and he enables the deaf to hear and the dumb to speak (7:31-37). He raises a young girl from the dead (5:22-24, 35-43). One woman who has suffered hemorrhage for twelve years is cured by merely touching Jesus' garment as he passes (5:25-34).

The following accounts of three miracles are particularly effective examples of Mark's narrative and style.

The first of these (5:1-20) tells of the exorcizing of demons from a Gadarene who dwells "among the tombs"—a man so strong and so violent that neither fetters nor chains can hold him. As soon as he sees Jesus, he worships him and addresses him as the "Son of the most high God." Jesus commands the "unclean spirit" to come out of the man and demands its name. The spirit answers: "My name is Legion; for we are many." The devils, as Mark now calls them, beg to be allowed to stay in the country and to be permitted to enter a herd of swine near-by. Jesus grants the request, and the possessed swine (about two thousand of them) rush headlong down a steep bank into the sea and are drowned. Some scholars believe this story to be a folktale; they point out that the conversation with demons and the belief that demons could enter swine are examples of "typical elaboration" found in folktales.[14] Inasmuch as swineherding was a rather abominable occupation in Jewish eyes (see Luke 15:15), it is possible that a derisive element (casting aspersion on the central theme) had entered the story of the miracle by the time Mark heard it.

Another famous miracle (7:24-30) takes place outside Galilee in the neighborhood of Tyre and Sidon. Here a Syrophoenician woman finds Jesus, falls at his feet, and begs him to cast a devil out of her daughter. Jesus at first refuses, saying to her (perhaps only half in earnest): "Let the children first be filled: for it is not meet to take the children's bread, and to cast it unto the dogs." (The implication is that he ought to minister to his own Jewish countrymen before aiding Gentiles.) The woman shrewdly replies: "Yes, Lord: yet the dogs under the table eat of the children's crumbs." Evidently pleased with her wit, Jesus grants her request: "For this saying go thy way; the devil is gone out of thy daughter." This incident reveals a certain sense of humor in Jesus and adds to our conception of his *human* nature.

At another time a man who is both deaf and tongue-tied is brought to Jesus to be cured:

And he [Jesus] took him aside from the multitude, and put his fingers into his ears, and he spit, and touched his tongue; And looking up to heaven, he sighed, and saith unto him, Ephphatha, that is, Be opened. And straightway his ears were opened, and the string of his tongue was loosed, and he spake plain. (7:33-35)

This passage, by the way, is a good example of several of Mark's stylistic traits: inclusion of striking details; frequent use of the historical present tense ("saith"); the practice of using and translating Aramaic words; and rapidity of movement ("straightway").

Rescues at Sea (4:35-41 and 6:45-52). Once as Jesus and his Disciples are crossing the Sea of Galilee in a small boat, a storm threatens to sink the vessel. Jesus is asleep at the time, and the Disciples awaken him with the words: "Master, carest thou not that we perish?" Jesus calms the wind and the waves by saying, "Peace, be still," and then rebukes the Disciples for their lack of faith. The Disciples, terrified, ask one another: "What manner of man is this, that even the wind and the sea obey him?"

On another occasion the Disciples are rowing a boat at night while Jesus is on shore. He sees them unable to make headway against contrary winds. He walks across the water toward them. When they see him walking on the surface of the sea, they cry out in fear, thinking that he is a spirit. He calms them with the famous words: "Be of good cheer: it is I; be not afraid." The wind subsides, and again the Disciples are amazed "beyond measure." This story has parallels "in Hellenistic literature, in the life of the Buddha, and in the lives of the saints." [15]

Feeding of the Thousands (6:30-44 and 8:1-10). Mark tells two stories which many Biblical scholars consider to be "doublets"—that is, two versions of the same event.*

In the first story, by embarking in a boat and sailing to a deserted place, Jesus and the Disciples try to escape from the crowds which have been following them. They are soon discovered, however, and a multitude of five thousand gathers.

---

* Compare the two stories of Moses' striking the rock (Ex. 17:1-7 and Num. 20:2-13).

"Moved with compassion toward them, because they were as sheep not having a shepherd," Jesus ignores his weariness and teaches them many things. Late in the day the Disciples urge him to send the people away to buy food; but Jesus replies: "Give ye them to eat." When he discovers that the only viands available are five small loaves and two fish, he "blesses" the loaves and fish, divides them, and has the Disciples distribute the pieces. There is enough to feed all the people gathered there; after everybody has eaten his fill, twelve basketfuls of fragments are left over.

In the second story (8:1-10), a crowd of four thousand has been with Jesus for three whole days without eating. He feeds them with *seven* loaves and "a few small fishes"; seven (instead of twelve) basketfuls of remains are gathered after the feeding.

If the accounts are indeed doublets, the presence of both may be explained by Mark's dependence on two sources for his material. Both may have been influenced by Old Testament legends about providing food by miraculous means: for example, Elijah's causing of the widow's meal and oil to be inexhaustible (I Kings 17:8-16), and Elisha's feeding of a hundred men with twenty loaves and some ears of corn (II Kings 4:42-44).[16]

PARABLES

Of the forty-one recognizable parables preserved in the Synoptic Gospels, Mark records only eight, one of which (The Growing Seed, 4:26-29) is peculiar to his Gospel.

Parables of the New Doctrine. In the first two parables recorded by Mark (2:21,22), Jesus indicates that his teachings are revolutionary, that they involve a wholly new concept of ethics and religion. To try simply to attach these to the old concepts would be like sewing a patch of new material onto an old garment: the garment would be further damaged by the patch. His teachings are also like new wine, which would burst old wineskins (old religious doctrines).

Parable of the Spread of the Word. The Parable of the Sower (4:3-20) compares the teachings of the Word of the Lord to the sowing of seed. Just as the results of the sowing vary according to the kinds of soil on which the seeds fall, so the effectiveness of the Word varies according to the receptivity and faithfulness of the hearers.

Parables of the Kingdom of God. The next two parables are concerned with "the Kingdom of God." * In the first (4:26-29) Jesus likens the Kingdom to seed which grows without human help and which eventually produces fruit. In the second (4:30-32) he compares the Kingdom to a grain of mustard seed which, though it is the smallest of seeds, grows into a large plant.

Parable of Religious Controversy. One parable was inspired by Jesus' controversy with the priests and scribes. The Parable of the Wicked Husbandmen (12:1-12) is an attack on the priests, the elders, and the scribes (11:27-28). This story is about a man who sent many servants, one after another, to receive payment from those who had leased his vineyard. Each servant was beaten or killed. Finally, the owner sent his own son, but the wicked husbandmen killed him, too. The parable obviously alludes to the mistreated prophets of the Old Testament (the servants), to Jesus himself (the son), and to the Jews (the lessors) who have refused to listen to God's messages brought by the prophets and Jesus.

Parables of the Second Coming. The last two parables in Mark are concerned with the Parousia (the Second Coming of Jesus). Jesus says that there will be signs to show when the time is near, just as the budding of the fig tree signals the approach of summer (13:28-29). In the Parable of the Watchful Servants (13:34-37) he compares himself to a householder going on a journey; all the servants (all men) should remain in constant readiness for the master's return.

DOCTRINAL TEACHINGS

Although Mark reproduces no sermons delivered by Jesus, he does record several of the Teacher's precepts about various religious and ethical matters.

Re-evaluation of Riches in the Light of Social Duty (10:17-27 and 12:41-44). Francis Bacon has said: "Prosperity is the blessing of the Old Testament; adversity is the blessing of the New." [17] The statement serves to emphasize Jesus' revolutionary attitude

---

* The phrase "the Kingdom of God" (or "the Kingdom of Heaven") as used in the Gospels has at least two different meanings. Sometimes it denotes a present reality among those who are dedicated to God. Elsewhere it seems to refer to an external future realm over which God will have established his perfect and undisputed reign. See *DB*, pp. 973-974.

toward money. On a number of other occasions he warns that possessions can very easily make a man forget the highest and most important things in life—self-sacrifice and complete devotion to God.

Mark tells the famous story (10:17-22) of the rich young man who runs up to Jesus, kneels reverently, and asks the Master what he must do to inherit eternal life. When Jesus reminds him of the Commandments, the young man says that he has obeyed them from his youth. Then Jesus tells him that he must do one more thing, namely, sell everything that he has and give to the poor, and the young man "went away grieved." The obvious moral is that this young man, though religious and law-abiding, is interested chiefly in his own happiness; until he loves his fellow-men enough to sacrifice his wealth for them, he does not deserve eternal life.

Jesus uses this incident as an occasion for a denunciation of riches. Mark attributes a striking hyperbole to Jesus: "It is easier for a camel to go through the eye of a needle, than for a rich man to enter into the Kingdom of God" (10:25). Jesus tells his Disciples that whoever wants to attain the Kingdom and to be rewarded with eternal life must forsake all worldly ambitions.

Another well-known incident (12:41-44) [18] concerns the "widow's mites": In Jerusalem Jesus watches the people contribute to the Temple treasury. The rich make large contributions, but a poor widow throws in two very small coins. Jesus declares that the widow has made the greatest donation, for she has cast in all she has, "even all her living," whereas the rich have given only a small part "of their abundance."

Respect for the Weak and Helpless (9:36-37,42; 10:13-16). Once the Disciples try to prevent some little children from approaching Jesus too closely, apparently fearing that the children would annoy the Master.[19] Jesus rebukes the Disciples: "Suffer the little children to come unto me, and forbid them not: for of such is the Kingdom of God" (10:14). It would be better, he says (9:42), for a man to be cast into the sea with a millstone around his neck than to cause a little child to sin.

A Redefinition of Discipleship (8:34-38; 9:33-35; 10:28-31, 35-45). A considerable percentage of Jesus' teachings in Mark's Gospel is directed to the Disciples, who find it difficult to grasp his message of self-sacrificial service to others. More than once he rebukes them for seeking personal glory. He warns them that his followers must learn self-denial and suffering, for he has come to bring spiritual rather than material values to men:

For whosoever will save his life shall lose it; but whosoever shall lose his life for my sake and the gospel's, the same shall save it. For what shall it profit a man, if he shall gain the whole world, and lose his own soul? (8:35-36)

When Jesus finds the Twelve disputing among themselves as to which one will be the greatest, he says to them: "If any man desire to be first, the same shall be last of all, and servant of all" (9:35). Still failing to understand, James and John request that they be allowed to sit, respectively, at his right and at his left hand in the new kingdom which he is going to establish. Once more Jesus tells them:

Whosoever will be great among you, shall be your minister [servant]: And whosoever of you will be the chiefest, shall be servant of all. For even the Son of man came not to be ministered unto, but to minister, and to give his life a ransom for many. (10:43-45)

CONTROVERSIES WITH SCRIBES, PHARISEES, HERODIANS, AND SADDUCEES

From the early days of his ministry Jesus is continually opposed by four classes of people: (1) scribes, who, as copyists of the Law (many of them are also Pharisees), consider themselves authorities on interpretation of the Law and on rabbinical traditions; (2) Pharisees, who hate Jesus for transcending the Law and for disregarding their interpretations of it; (3) Herodians, who fear that Jesus may undermine the authority of their tetrarch; and (4) Sadducees, who feel that Jesus is a threat to their vested interests and to their authority as civil and religious leaders of the Jewish people. On ordinary occasions the scribes and Pharisees were intensely nationalistic and scorned the Herodians and the Sadducees as collaborators with the Romans, and the scribes and Pharisees also differed violently with the Sadducees on interpretations of the Law. But fear makes strange bedfellows, for all unite in opposition to Jesus.

Often an altercation with one of these groups provides Jesus with an opportunity to teach a moral or religious lesson.

Friction in Galilee and Perea (2:3–3:6; 3:22-27; 7:1-23; 8:11-15; 10:2-9). The first bit of friction is with some of the scribes.* Jesus says to a man stricken with palsy (paralysis): "Son, thy sins be forgiven thee" (2:5). Silently ("reasoning in their hearts") the scribes accuse Jesus of blasphemy; for only God, they know, can forgive sins.[20] Perceiving their sentiments, Jesus asks then whether it is easier to forgive a man's sins or to cure him of paralysis. He amazes them all by curing the paralytic.

Very soon after this encounter Jesus antagonizes scribes and Pharisees by dining with "publicans and sinners" (2:15-17).† He confounds his antagonists by telling them that, as it is the sick and not the healthy who need a doctor, so it is the sinful and not the righteous who need his aid toward repentance.

Somewhat later, Pharisees rebuke Jesus and his Disciples for plucking and eating grain on the Sabbath, an act which, according to their interpretation of the Law, is "work" and which is therefore prohibited on that day. Jesus recalls to them that David, God's beloved servant, broke the Law by eating the forbidden shewbread when he was hungry (I Sam. 21:1-6), and besides, Jesus says, "The sabbath was made for man, and not man for the sabbath" (2:27).

Again, some Pharisees accuse him of lawbreaking when he cures a man's withered hand on the Sabbath. He asks them whether it is better to do good or to do evil on the Sabbath, to save life or to kill (3:4). They refuse to answer him and begin to plot with the Herodians against Jesus' life.

The next controversy is with scribes, who contend that Jesus' ability to cast out devils is the result of his being a servant of Beelzebub.‡ Jesus refutes their contention by pointing out that such a procedure would amount to civil war in Satan's realm: "How can Satan cast out Satan? And if a kingdom be divided against itself, that kingdom cannot stand" (3:24-25).

---

* Luke's version of the story (5:21) refers to "scribes and Pharisees."

† The "sinners" were sinners in the eyes of the Pharisees because they disregarded the strict observance of the Mosaic Law (*DB*, p. 966). Dining together is often mentioned in both Old and New Testaments—nearly always as an indication of intimacy between the diners.

‡ *Beelzebub* was apparently at one time the name of some pagan deity. By New Testament times that term had become a name for a devil—*the* devil, or Satan. See Davies, *Abingdon Bible Commentary*, pp. 1004-05.

The conflict between Jesus and the scribes grows so heated that apparently the scribes in Jerusalem feel it advisable to send an investigating committee (7:1).[21] Along with some Pharisees, they find fault with the Disciples for eating with "unwashen hands"—that is, for ignoring certain prescribed ceremonial ablutions. Jesus launches a vigorous counterattack: he brands the scribes and Pharisees as hypocrites and quotes both a prophet (Isa. 29:13) and the Law (Ex. 20:12, 21:1, and Deut. 5:16) to confound them. He says (7:6-9, 18-23) that these hypocrites are more interested in obeying man's traditions than in keeping God's laws and that a man is defiled *not* by what goes into him (such as "unclean" food or food eaten with "unclean" hands) but by what comes out of him (such as evil thoughts and deeds).

Twice before Jesus reaches Jerusalem, Pharisees "tempt" (test) him in an effort to find fault or contradiction. They ask for a "sign" or miracle (8:11-13). Jesus flatly refuses: he has performed enough miracles to convince all unprejudiced people of his divine power. He warns the Disciples against the "leaven" (hypocrisy or lack of faith and understanding)[22] of the Pharisees and the Herodians. After he has entered Perea (the region east of the Jordan and directly across from the Holy City) the Pharisees tempt him again by asking whether a man should ever divorce his wife (10:2). If Jesus says no, as they expect him to do, they can charge him with denying the Mosaic Law (Deut. 24:1); but Jesus is too shrewd to be trapped. He asks them for Moses' ruling on the matter, and they say that the lawgiver permitted a man to set his wife aside with a bill of divorcement. Jesus' rejoinder is that Moses' rule was a concession to man's hardheartedness, but that God never intended married couples to be divorced.[23] To his Disciples Jesus explains that if either a man or a woman remarries after being divorced, he or she is committing adultery.

Clashes in Jerusalem (11:15-19, 27-33; 12:1-40; 14:1-2). Jesus' first act upon entering the Holy City is to visit the Temple. Inside he sees money-changers and merchants gathered to prey upon the many pilgrims coming to Jerusalem to celebrate the Passover. In great wrath Jesus overthrows the tables of the greedy (and perhaps dishonest) merchants, accusing them thus: "Is it not written, My house shall be called of all nations the house of prayer? but ye have made it a den of thieves" (11:17).[24] His actions and words antagonize the scribes, the Sadducees, and the chief priests, who have been anticipating a tidy profit from the transactions in the Temple. This attack on their financial interests is the immediate cause of the accusations which lead to Christ's trial and execution.[25]

On the following day the scribes, the elders, and the chief priests confront him in the Temple and demand to know by what authority he has made such a disturbance. Jesus replies: "I will also ask of you one question, and answer me, and I will tell you by what authority I do these things. The baptism of John, was it from heaven, or of men? answer me" (11:29-30). His antagonists refuse to answer, because they know that if they say, "From heaven," then he will ask why they did not believe John; but if they say, "Of men," then the people, who regard John as a prophet, will be outraged. Jesus, in turn, refuses to answer their query.

Jesus tells the Parable of the Wicked Husbandmen (12:1-12). The priests and scribes understand it as an attack upon them, and they long for revenge, but refrain from action because they fear the people.

They send to Jesus some Pharisees and Herodians, who once again try to trap him by asking him whether it is lawful to pay tribute to Caesar (12:13-17). If Jesus answers yes, he will arouse the enmity of the people; but if he answers no, then he will bring down on his head the wrath of the Roman authorities. Adroitly Jesus evades the issue by requesting a coin and asking whose image appears on it. When his tempters answer, "Caesar's," he retorts, "Render to Caesar the things that are Caesar's, and to God the things that are God's."

Next the high and mighty Sadducees (who do not believe in the return of the dead) attempt to entangle Christ (12:18-27). Suppose, they ask him, that a woman should marry and outlive each of seven different husbands and then herself die: in the afterlife, whose wife would she be? Jesus answers that his questioners know neither the Scriptures nor the power of God. Those who rise from the dead, he says, shall neither marry nor be given in marriage, because they are "as the angels which are in heaven." Furthermore, he continues, there is a resurrection, for did not God tell Moses: "I am the God of Abraham, and the

God of Isaac, and the God of Jacob"? Since the Jews believed that these patriarchs were still alive, Jesus argues that they must therefore have been resurrected.

A scribe then asks which is the greatest commandment. Jesus replies: "And thou shalt love the Lord thy God with all thy heart, and with all thy soul, and with all thy mind, and with all thy strength: this is the first commandment. And the second is like, namely this, Thou shalt love thy neighbour as thyself" (12:30-31).*

Jesus now assumes the offensive and attacks the scribes' practice of religion as hypocritical. They seek the admiration of the public by doing such things as wearing ornate clothes ("the garb of honor" [26]), sitting in the chief seats in the synagogues, and reciting long prayers; but at the same time by their greed they have devoured widows' houses (12:38-40).

The hostilities between Jesus and his opponents reach a climax about two days before the great festival of the Passover. The chief priests and the scribes plot how they may seize him secretly, for they fear an uprising of the people if they act openly (14:1-2). At length they bribe Judas to betray Jesus at a convenient time (14:10-11).[27]

REVELATION OF MESSIAHSHIP AND PREDICTIONS
OF THE CRUCIFIXION (8:27-33; 9:31; 10:32-34)

Reviewing Mark's account of Jesus' ministry, we find an important turning point in his revelation to the Apostles that he is the Messiah (8:27-30); † from this time onward the shadow of the Cross lies athwart his path.[28] The revelation comes at Caesarea Philippi, where he asks the Apostles whom people

---

* In Matthew (22:40) Jesus adds: "On these two commandments hang all the law and the prophets." He takes the two commandments from Deut. 6:4 and Lev. 19:18.

† It should be remembered that for several centuries the Palestinian Jews had been expecting a Messiah (whose coming had been predicted by several prophets)—a military conqueror who would defeat their enemies and set up a temporal kingdom. In the time of Jesus the Zealots especially entertained hopes for such a leader. Accepting Jesus as the promised Messiah, Christians from the earliest days have reinterpreted the traditions and prophecies about Messiahship, considering Jesus a *spiritual* Messiah and his kingdom a *spiritual* kingdom. In this way his coming fulfilled for them the old prophecies.

believe him to be. They answer that some say he is John the
Baptist; others, Elias (Elijah); * still others, one of the prophets.
Then he asks the Disciples: "But whom say ye that I am?" Im-
petuously, as usual, Peter answers, "Thou art the Christ." Jesus
charges them to tell nobody.

Three times in quick succession (8:31-33, 9:31, and 10:32-34)
Jesus predicts his trial, death, and Resurrection. Mark's purpose
in recording these predictions is doubtless to show that Jesus
foresees and accepts the sufferings he is about to endure.[29] The
Disciples still do not grasp the significance of these announce-
ments.

THE TRANSFIGURATION (9:2-8)

After Peter's "confession" of faith in Jesus as the Christ, the
Master's divine nature is reaffirmed in the Transfiguration. Jesus
takes Peter, James, and John with him up on a high mountain
and is there *transfigured* before them: his clothes become "shining, exceeding white as snow; so as no fuller on earth can white
them." † Moses and Elijah appear and talk with him.[30] Peter is
so overcome that he does not know what to say; but apparently
he feels that the occasion demands some sort of speech, for he
does address Jesus. His suggestion is the inept kind of reaction
that we might expect under the circumstances: "Master, it is good
for us to be here: and let us make three tabernacles [booths];
one for thee, and one for Moses, and one for Elias." Christ does
not reply, but a cloud overshadows the scene, and a voice from
the cloud declares: "This is my beloved Son: hear him." ‡ Suddenly the Transfiguration is over, and Jesus is left alone with
the three Disciples.

THE TRIUMPHAL ENTRY INTO JERUSALEM (11:1-10)

Jesus continues his ministry on a journey through Perea, en
route to Jerusalem, where he and the Twelve will celebrate the
Passover. After crossing the Jordan and passing through Jericho,

---

* Malachi (4:5) had prophesied that Elijah would reappear to announce
the advent of the Messiah.

† Compare Moses' appearance after his descent from Mt. Sinai (Ex.
34:29-35).

‡ Compare the voice at Jesus' baptism (Mark 1:11) and also the declaration of the Roman soldier at the Crucifixion (Mark 15:39).

the group reaches Bethphage and Bethany, suburbs of Jerusalem. Now the Master sends two of the Disciples ahead to procure a colt (of an ass), which he says they will find tied near the entrance to a certain village and which the owner will willingly give to them when they say, "The Lord hath need of him." All happens as Jesus has predicted. Then he makes his triumphal entry into Jerusalem, while the people of the city, acknowledging his Messiahship, spread their garments and branches of trees in the path before him and cry: "Hosanna; Blessed is he that cometh in the name of the Lord: Blessed be the kingdom of our father David, that cometh in the name of the Lord: Hosanna in the highest." * (This event is commemorated in the annual Christian celebration of Palm Sunday, the Sunday before Easter.)

THE "LITTLE APOCALYPSE" (CH. 13)

In the thirteenth chapter of Mark, Jesus predicts the destruction of Jerusalem, the end of the world, and his own Second Coming. The prediction is occasioned by an Apostle's admiration of the Temple buildings in Jerusalem; Jesus prophesies that these will all be razed. When Peter, Andrew, James, and John ask him when the terrible event will happen, Jesus tells them that many other things must come to pass before the fall of Jerusalem. There will be impostors who will claim to be the Christ, and there will be "wars and rumours of wars." Men will betray their own brothers and fathers, and the faithful followers of Jesus will suffer persecution. Still the end will not be then, for "the gospel must first be published among all nations. . . . But when ye shall see the abomination of desolation . . . standing where it ought not [the desecration of the Temple by Titus?] . . ., then let them that be in Judaea flee to the mountains." There will be great suffering and destruction, and then "the sun shall be darkened, and the moon shall not give her light, And the stars of heaven shall fall, and the powers that are in heaven shall be shaken" (13:24-25). After that, Christ will come again in all his glory to gather up his elect from the uttermost parts of the earth. Neither man nor angel yet knows when that hour will be. On the other hand, "Verily . . . this generation shall not pass, till all these

* Jesus' peaceful and humble "entry" is in striking contrast to the Jewish expectation that the Messiah would enter the capital city with much pomp and fanfare, as a mighty military hero.

things be done." Jesus issues a stern warning to the Apostles to pray and to be prepared for the Second Coming. "And what I say unto you I say unto all, Watch."

THE LAST SUPPER (14:12-26)

Jesus and the Twelve begin preparations for the celebration of Passover and the feast of Unleavened Bread. This important Jewish festival, it will be remembered, is a sort of Independence Day,[31] commemorating the escape of the Jews from the Egyptians in the days of Moses. Jesus sends two of his Disciples into Jerusalem to secure a suitable place for the customary meal of bread and wine.* Following Jesus' directions, the Disciples find "a large upper room furnished and prepared" in the home of an unnamed man. Here Jesus and the Disciples gather for the Last Supper. It is a dramatic moment when Jesus announces that he is to be betrayed by one of those present, and the Disciples ask him one by one, "Is it I?" In Mark's account Jesus does not divulge the identity of the traitor, but repeats that it is one of the Twelve, and he says that it would have been better for that man if he had never been born.

He proceeds to break the bread and to pass the cup of wine, proclaiming that the former is his body and the latter his blood, "of the new testament, which is shed for many" (14:24). This occasion is, of course, the origin of the holiest of Christian sacraments, the Eucharist, or Holy Communion.

After singing a hymn, the group leaves the upper room and goes out to the Mount of Olives, a short distance outside the city of Jerusalem.

ARREST, TRIALS, CRUCIFIXION, AND BURIAL (14:27–15:47)

After the Last Supper the conspiracy against Jesus proceeds with rapidity. From that event to the time of his burial is a matter of only twenty-four hours.

---

* One should be aware of the distinction between the Jewish feast (consisting largely of paschal lamb and bitter herbs, accompanied by religious ceremonies) and the Christian celebration of the Last Supper (which is supposed to have taken place during the same season). The Synoptics apparently confuse the two festivals; John does not. Many early churchmen, from St. Paul onwards, have tried to find a symbolic resemblance, but historical-minded students of the Bible and most Jewish readers do not regard the feasts as identical. See Grant, *IB*, VII, 867 and 876.

Arrest in Gethsemane (14:27-52). On the Mount of Olives, Jesus again predicts to the Disciples his death and Resurrection, and he promises to precede the Disciples into Galilee. He foretells, too, that the Disciples will desert him before the night is over. Impulsive as always, Peter vehemently declares that he will not forsake his Master even though all the others do so. Jesus prophesies that Peter will deny him thrice before the cock crows twice. Then he goes with the Twelve to the Garden of Gethsemane (on one side of the Mount of Olives). Here he tells them to keep watch while he will be praying. Peter, James, and John are led a short distance from the others. Jesus, "sore amazed," prays that the bitter cup of suffering which he knows is before him be taken away, if it be God's will. Three times he returns to the favored Disciples, only to find them asleep; the first two times he chides them, but on his third return, after bidding them, "Rise up," he says, "Let us go"—it is now too late for them to watch, for his betrayer has arrived.

Judas Iscariot appears with a great mob armed with swords and staves. He advances and kisses Jesus in order to identify him for the mob. One of Jesus' followers cuts off the ear of the high priest's servant.* When the mob seizes Jesus, all his followers flee.†

Trial before the Sanhedrin (14:53-72). Now Jesus is led before the Sanhedrin, which acts as a court of judgment. At first nobody can be found who will testify against the defendant, but soon perjuring witnesses bring false charges. Jesus refuses to say anything in answer to their accusations. At length the high priest ‡ asks, "Art thou the Christ, the Son of the Blessed?" On receiving an affirmative answer, he tears his clothes and says that no witnesses are necessary, for, he asserts, Jesus has spoken blasphemously in the hearing of all. The court unanimously declares Jesus guilty and deserving of the death penalty.[32]

---

* Luke (22:51) says that Jesus restored the servant's ear. John (18:10) gives the servant's name as Malchus and identifies the one who cut off the servant's ear as Simon Peter.

† Here (14:51-52) occurs the controversial incident of the young man wearing a "linen cloth," one of Jesus' followers, who is seized by the mob but escapes naked, leaving his cloth behind him. Some commentators have concluded that the young man was John Mark.

‡ Identified by Matthew (26:57) as Caiaphas.

Peter is in the crowd outside the courtroom. He is approached by a maidservant of the high priest, who accuses him of being one of Jesus' companions; fearful for his own safety, he denies her charge. The cock crows once. Again a servant links him with Jesus, and once more Peter denies his Lord. A little later some of the people insist that, since he is a Galilean (as his speech indicates), he must be a follower of Jesus. Peter curses and swears: "I know not this man of whom ye speak." The cock crows again. Remembering Jesus' prediction, Peter is overcome with remorse and weeps (14:72).

Trial before Pontius Pilate (15:1-15). Lacking the authority to inflict the death penalty, the Sanhedrin sends Jesus the next morning before Pontius Pilate, the Roman procurator of Judea. The chief priests accuse the prisoner of many transgressions, but again Jesus remains silent. Now, it was the custom to release one Jewish prisoner each year at the Passover festival. Pilate, who regards Jesus as harmless, asks the people whether they wish Jesus set free, but, incited by the priests, the people cry out for the release of Barabbas, an insurrectionist and murderer. Pilate next asks what he should do with Jesus, and the mob shouts, "Crucify him." Pilate reluctantly consents.

Crucifixion and Burial (15:16-47). The Roman soldiers clothe Jesus in purple, place a crown of thorns on his head, and mockingly hail him as King of the Jews. One Simon of Cyrene is forced to help him bear the Cross to Golgotha, and there Jesus is crucified. After suffering for six hours, Jesus cries out in a loud voice, "My God, my God, why has thou forsaken me?" and dies. A Roman centurion, observing, is so deeply moved that he exclaims: "Truly this man was the Son of God" (15:39).

Joseph of Arimathaea, "an honourable counsellor," requests and receives the body of Jesus, wraps it in fine linen, places it in a sepulchre hewn out of rock, and rolls a large stone to close the door of the sepulchre.

RESURRECTION AND ASCENSION (CH. 16)

The Crucifixion and burial take place on the sixth day of the week.* At sunrise on the first day of the new week there come

---

* Mark makes no mention of what happens on the seventh day, the Sabbath.

to the tomb Mary, the mother of the Apostle James "the Less" and Joses; Mary Magdalene; * and Salome, the wife of Zebedee and mother of James and John. Bringing spices to anoint the body of Jesus, they wonder who will help them roll away the stone from the door of the tomb. To their great surprise, they discover that the stone has already been removed. They enter the sepulchre and see a "young man" (an angel?) clothed in a long white garment.

And he saith unto them, Be not affrighted: ye seek Jesus of Nazareth, which was crucified: he is risen; he is not here: behold the place where they laid him. . . . And they went out quickly, and fled from the sepulchre; for they trembled and were amazed: neither said they anything to any man; for they were afraid. (16:6,8)

In the most ancient manuscripts, the Gospel of Mark ends with this verse. Nearly all Biblical scholars agree that verses 9-20 are an epilogue added by some redactor.[33] These verses tell of Jesus' appearing to Mary Magdalene, to two of the Disciples on one occasion, and to the Eleven (Judas, of course, being no longer among the Disciples) at a later time. He gives them the great missionary command: "Go ye into all the world, and preach the gospel to every creature." He gives them power to cast out devils and to heal the sick. After that he is received into heaven and sits at God's right hand. The Disciples obey his command, preaching everywhere, "the Lord working with them, and confirming the word with signs following."

---

* Mary Magdalene (mentioned first by Mark in 15:40) is a Galilean woman from whom Jesus has cast out seven devils (Luke 8:2) and who has become one of his most devoted followers. The later tradition which depicts her as a woman of ill repute is "unjustified." See Buttrick, *IB*, VII, 611.

3

The Gospel According to Matthew: The Fullest Account of the Life and Teachings of Jesus

Ernest Renan has called St. Matthew's Gospel (the fortieth book of the Bible) "the most important book which has ever been written." [1] E. F. Scott says: "It has been accepted in all times as the authoritative account of the life of Christ, the fundamental document of the Christian religion." [2] For several reasons this Gospel is generally regarded as the most significant of the four: (1) The arrangement of its material makes it the most suitable as a handbook of instruction. (2) It contains the fullest account of Jesus' life and teachings. (3) For all Christian groups, it seems to reflect the greatest catholicity of outlook. (4) It is the most ecclesiastical and best meets the needs of church life. [3]

AUTHORSHIP, SOURCES, PLACE AND DATE, LANGUAGE

There has been much controversy over the authorship, sources, date and place of composition, and original language of this Gospel.

Authorship. The tradition ascribing the book to the Disciple Matthew is very ancient. Eusebius quotes the second-century prelate Papias as saying: "Matthew composed the oracles [or sayings] in the Hebrew language, but everyone interpreted them as he was able." [4] Nobody knows whether Papias was referring to our Gospel of Matthew, to a book of *logia* ("sayings") supposedly collected by the tax-gathering Apostle, or to some other Gospel no longer extant. The weight of evidence, however, is strongly against the Apostle's authorship of our Gospel. In the first place, the book was almost certainly not composed by an eyewitness, for an eyewitness would not find it necessary to use a written source. In the second place, it is written in Greek, is derived from Greek sources, and is addressed at least partially to a Gentile church; the Disciple Matthew almost certainly was a Hebrew. And finally, in all probability the Gospel was composed at a time well after the deaths of all the Disciples. About the only evidence in favor of Matthew's authorship is his relative obscurity as an Apostle—if he did not write the book, why would posterity choose one of the minor Apostles to attribute it to? Most scholars today consider the Gospel anonymous.

Sources. The author, whoever he was,* made skillful use of several sources. Most scholars believe that, for the narrative portions of his book, he relied principally on the Gospel according to Mark. Of the 661 verses in the earlier Gospel, 600 reappear in Matthew.[5] In narrative passages Matthew usually follows Mark's order and omits few events. He does, however, omit some details and he changes many verses. Some of the omissions and changes are made for the sake of improving the style; others are made for doctrinal reasons: (1) to improve the portrayal of Jesus as perfect in goodness and power—for example, Matthew omits Jesus' harshness to the leper (compare Matt. 8:2-3 with Mark 1:43) and Jesus' displays of anger (compare Matt. 12:10-14 and 19:13-15 with Mark 3:5 and 10:14); (2) to defend the honor of the Disciples (compare Matt. 16:5-12 with Mark 8:14-21); and (3) to make certain teachings more applicable to the Christian community (compare Matt. 19:3-9 with Mark 10:2-12).[6] Often Matthew abbreviates a Marcan passage, omitting graphic and intimate details, in order to leave space for other matters.[7]

It has been noted above that the Gospel of Mark records relatively few of the teachings, or "sayings," of Jesus. For those, both Matthew and Luke rely on another source, now known as "Q" (see p. 13). According to W. O. Sypherd, about 250 verses in Matthew may be traced to that source.[8] Some scholars have believed that Papias' remark, quoted above, referred to the Q document; but Papias said that the "oracles" were in Hebrew (by which he meant Aramaic). The Q document used by Matthew and Luke, however, was written in Greek; perhaps it was a

---

* For the sake of convenience, we shall hereafter refer to this author as Matthew, irrespective of his real identity.

Greek translation of the Aramaic "oracles" mentioned by Papias. Matthew cleverly weaves the sayings from Q into the narrative framework provided by Mark.

A third major source, used only by Matthew, is now known as "M"; from it the Evangelist drew about 300 verses.[9] The passages from M are concerned primarily with Jewish law and make no attempt to appeal to Gentiles; M represents the "extreme Judaizing party at Jerusalem." [10]

St. Matthew uses the Septuagint (Greek) version of the Old Testament for many passages concerned with Hebrew Law and prophecy.

The historian Josephus speaks of public registers of Hebrew genealogies.[11] In all probability Matthew had one of these registers and drew on it for the genealogy of Jesus (1:1-16).

Many incidents peculiar to Matthew's Gospel (for example, the story of the Wise Men, 2:1-12) are believed to have been derived from "floating" traditions, preserved orally for several decades.

Place and Date. Nobody has been able to establish the place or the date of composition of Matthew. As for the place, most commentators feel that Antioch in Syria is the most likely, because that city was an important center of Christianity, the headquarters of Christian activity,[12] and the "meeting place of both Jewish and Gentile influences." [13] Other places suggested are Edessa and Apamea in eastern Syria [14] and various places in Palestine.[15] As regards the date of composition, the Roman Catholics and most of the liberal and secular scholars accept the estimate, "just before 90 A.D." [16] A date late in the century is indicated by these seven factors: (1) Matthew's use of Mark (see p. 13); (2) the church organization as reflected in Matthew; (3) apparent references to the persecution of Christians under Domitian (A.D. 81-96) (4) apparent references to the fall of Jerusalem; (5) the exalted praise for the Apostles; (6) the use of many phrases such as "to this time" and "unto this day" (27:8); and (7) expressions of disappointment over the delay of Jesus' Second Coming.[17] The author's failure to show knowledge of St. Paul's letters (circulated about A.D. 90) suggests a date late in the 80's.[18] In A.D. 96 Clement of Rome wrote a letter which seems to refer to this Gospel.[19]

Language. Matthew's Gospel, as we know it, was written in *Koiné*—the vulgar Greek dialect current over the Mediterranean world in the first century A.D. The theory held by Torrey and others that some or all of the Gospels were originally written in Aramaic is unconvincing with regard to Matthew. As S. E. Johnson points out, to assume the rendering of Greek sources (Mark, Q, and the Septuagint) into Aramaic and then back into *Koiné* is a needless multiplication of hypotheses.[20]

AIMS OF MATTHEW

As we have seen, Mark seems to have addressed his Gospel to the Roman Gentiles and to have aimed primarily at relating the deeds of Jesus. Addressing a different audience, the Jews and Gentiles of Asia Minor, Matthew had other, more specific aims: (1) to present a fuller biography of Jesus, beginning with his birth and ending with his reappearance to the Disciples after his Resurrection; (2) to record the *teachings* of Jesus, to a large extent ignored by Mark; (3) to convince the Jewish people that Jesus was the Messiah descended from David and promised by the prophets of the Old Testament, that Jesus had come to fulfill and extend—not to overthrow—the ancient Jewish Law, and perhaps that the destruction of Jerusalem by the Romans had been a direct result of the Jewish rejection of Jesus;[21] and (4) to persuade the Gentiles that Jesus was the Messiah for all the peoples of the world. The genealogy, the oft-repeated references to the Law and the prophets, and the frequent allusions (without explanation) to Jewish customs—all these passages have led scholars to emphasize the intention of Matthew to appeal to the Jews; and it must be admitted that the Gospel represents Jesus as saying that he came "but unto the lost sheep of the house of Israel" (15:24) and as directing his Disciples to heal and preach to those same "lost sheep" (10:6). In other passages, however, Matthew implies that Jesus' message is for the Gentiles rather than the Jews, for the latter have rejected him (see 8:11-12 and 21:43). Furthermore, Jesus commands his Apostles to preach the Gospel to the whole world and to make disciples of all nations (24:14 and 28:19).[22]

ORGANIZATION AND STYLE

Even a cursory reading will impress one with the fact that Matthew was more consciously concerned with matters of organization and literary style than Mark was.

In the first place, Matthew's book is far more carefully planned than Mark's. Whereas the shorter Gospel begins and ends abruptly, Matthew opens with a "positive beginning" at the birth of Jesus and systematically proceeds to a "preconceived conclusion." [23] Although he follows Mark's narrative order, Matthew's "framework is a marvelous combination of the chronological and the topical." [24] The teachings derived from Q are logically rearranged so as to form five unified discourses; these are set into the Marcan narrative, and each discourse closes with the formula: "And it came to pass, when Jesus had ended these sayings, . . ." (7:28). For these five major blocks, each made up of narrative plus discourse (Chs. 3–7, 8–10, 11–13, 14–18, and 19–25), Matthew supplies an introduction (Chs. 1–2) relating the ancestry, birth, and early childhood of Jesus, and a conclusion (Chs. 26–28) containing accounts of Jesus' trial, Crucifixion, Resurrection, and reappearance in Galilee.

Matthew is a more economical writer than Mark. He deletes or condenses Mark's copious details, thereby sacrificing vividness for succinctness and proportion.

Among Matthew's merits as a writer are aptness in choice of words, and the use of balance, parallelism, contrast, and repetition. He gains a great deal from abundant use of dialogue and monologue, especially when he allows Jesus to speak for himself.[25]

Other noteworthy features of his style and technique are (1) a fondness for the numbers 3, 5, and 7 (three appearances of the angel to Joseph, Peter's three denials of Jesus, division of teachings into five discourses, seven loaves of bread, seven woes [in Ch. 23], and so on); (2) the use of formulas and catchwords, such as "The Kingdom of Heaven is like . . ." and "that it might be fulfilled"; (3) the presence of a strong apocalyptic element, especially evident in the parables of the Ten Virgins and the Talents; and (4) ecclesiastical interest (only Matthew among Gospel authors uses the word *church*—perhaps to mean "kingdom").[26]

A total of 436 verses or parts of verses of Matthew appear in no other Gospel.[27] Most of these passages fall under one or another of the following headings: (1) brief additions to Mark, Q, or M; (2) the Sermon on the Mount (principally from M); (3) some quotations from the Old Testament; (4) formulas and transitional expressions added by Matthew himself; and (5) incidents and narratives of considerable length relating to the Nativity, the events of Passion Week, and the Resurrection (much of this fifth group, according to some scholars, is of a legendary nature and was probably derived from oral tradition).[28]

The most significant narrative passages peculiar to Matthew are the following: (1) certain details about the Nativity: the Birth, the visit of the Wise Men, the flight of the Holy Family into Egypt, the slaughter of the innocents, and the Family's return to Nazareth; (2) certain stories about Jesus' baptism and ministry: John's hesitation to baptize Jesus, Peter's walking on the water, and the appearance of the coin in the fish's mouth; (3) certain stories relating to the trial, Crucifixion, and Resurrection: Judas' taking of the thirty pieces of silver, the death of Judas, the dream of Pilate's wife, Pilate's washing his hands, the earthquake and the apparition of saints after the Crucifixion, the setting of a guard to watch the sepulchre, the removal of the stone from the entrance to the tomb, and the bribing of the soldiers.[29]

The most significant *teachings* of Jesus recorded only by Matthew are the Sermon on the Mount and the ten parables which have no counterpart in Luke or Mark.

The two most noteworthy passages in Mark which were ignored by Matthew are those concerning the widow's mites (Mark 12:41-44) and the Ascension (Mark 16:19-20).

INTRODUCTION: GENEALOGY, BIRTH, AND CHILDHOOD (1-2:23)*

Matthew traces the ancestry of Jesus all the way from Abraham down through forty-two generations. Some of the more memorable ancestors are Isaac, Jacob, Judah, Boaz and Ruth, David, Solomon, Hezekiah, and Josiah. It is a remarkable fact that, according to Matthew, the "blood royal" is transmitted to Jesus through Joseph, the husband of Mary; yet Matthew himself, Luke, and other leaders of Christian tradition maintain that Jesus was conceived by the Holy Spirit and born of the Virgin Mary and so had none of Joseph's blood in his veins. Matthew's genealogy, therefore, has been called a legal, rather than a biological, one.[30]

* Events and teachings already covered in Mark will be given only the barest mention or will be omitted altogether. A similar policy will be followed in the summaries of the Gospels of Luke and John, below.

The Gospel tells us that when Joseph discovers Mary to be pregnant before he has known her physically, he resolves to divorce her quietly. An angel appears, however, and informs him that Mary is still a virgin; that she is to bear a son; and that that son will be named Jesus, because he will "save" people from the consequences of their sins.*

Next Matthew tells the familiar but ever fascinating story of the Wise Men (2:1-12). Led from the east by a star of great magnitude, these Magi seek the newborn "King of the Jews" in Jerusalem. When Herod the Great hears of their search, he is considerably perturbed.[31] He calls the Magi to him, encourages their quest, and asks them to bring him news of the babe if they find it, because he says he wants to go and worship it, too. The Wise Men find Jesus in Bethlehem; they open their treasures and offer the Christ-child gifts of gold, frankincense, and myrrh, thus initiating the custom of giving presents on Christmas. Warned by an angel, they do not report to King Herod.

Joseph, too, is warned by an angel and flees with Jesus and Mary into Egypt. Fearful for his throne, Herod orders that all male children of the region who are two years old or younger be killed; this is the infamous "slaughter of the innocents." After Herod's death, Joseph and his family return from Egypt, but settle in the town of Nazareth in Galilee, far from Bethlehem, for Joseph fears Archelaus, Herod's successor in Judea.

BAPTISM AND TEMPTATION (3:13–4:11)

Like Mark, Matthew records John the Baptist's preparations for Jesus' ministry. When Jesus offers himself for baptism, John hesitates, saying, "I have need to be baptized of thee, and comest thou to me?" The implication, of course, is that Jesus is sinless and therefore does not need to have his sins washed away. Jesus insists, however, and is baptized.

Afterward the Holy Spirit leads Jesus into the wilderness, where he is tempted by the devil. Here Matthew, unlike Mark, goes into detail. For "forty" days and nights Jesus lives without food. Satan tempts him to turn stones into bread, and Jesus replies: "Man shall not live by bread alone. . . ." This trial prob-

---

* The name *Jesus* is the Greek form of Joshua, which literally means "Yahweh is salvation." In Matthew there is a pun: in Hebrew *yôshîá* means "shall save" (Johnson, *IB*, VII, 255).

ably is meant to symbolize bodily temptations in general. Next Satan takes Jesus to the pinnacle of the Temple and urges him to cast himself safely down—perhaps to make Jesus test God's protective power; again Jesus refuses. A third time Satan tempts him by offering him all the kingdoms of the world if he will worship the devil instead of God; this offer obviously symbolizes the temptation of worldly glory and power. Jesus, of course, refuses to be led astray and banishes Satan; angels come and minister unto him.

THE SERMON ON THE MOUNT (CHS. 5–7)*

Seated on an unnamed mountain, Jesus delivers his first major discourse, which is almost universally acknowledged to be the noblest and loftiest ethical code ever devised. This is the Law of the New Covenant, which stresses inward, individual goodness. Time after time Jesus emphasizes that he has come not to abolish the old Law and prophets but to fulfill and reinterpret them. Repeatedly he says, in effect, "The old Law says such and such, but I say unto you . . ." Each time he upholds the traditional Law but transcends it. For example, he quotes the Seventh Commandment, "Thou shalt not commit adultery," and then adds, "But I say unto you, That whosoever looketh on a woman to lust after her hath committed adultery with her already in his heart" (5:28). He preaches against ostentatious praying and almsgiving. He urges men not to be anxious about food, drink, clothing, and the like, for God knows that they need such things and will provide them, "But seek ye first the kingdom of God, and his righteousness; and all these things shall be added unto you" (6:33). "Lay up for yourselves treasures in heaven, where neither moth nor rust doth corrupt, and where thieves do not break through nor steal: For where your treasure is, there will your heart be also" (6:20-21).

Among the familiar passages in the Sermon on the Mount are the Beatitudes (5:3-12),† beginning with "Blessed are the poor in spirit: for theirs is the kingdom of heaven. . . .; the Lord's Prayer (6:9-13) ‡: "Our Father who art in heaven, Hallowed be

---

* A shorter version of some of the material in the Sermon on the Mount appears in Luke 6:20-49.

† For a shorter and less familiar version, see Luke 6:20-23.

‡ A shorter version of the Lord's Prayer appears in Luke 11:2-4.

thy name . . ."; and the Golden Rule (7:12): * "Therefore all things whatsoever ye would that men should do to you, do ye even so to them: for this is the law and the prophets."

THE APPOINTMENT OF PETER AS THE FOUNDATION OF CHRIST'S CHURCH (16:16-20)

Only the Gospel of Matthew records a certain pronouncement of Jesus which has become "perhaps the most debated" passage in the Bible.[32] After Peter has made his "confession" that Jesus is the Christ (reported also by Mark, 8:29), the Master blesses him and says:

Thou art Peter,† and upon this rock I will build my church; and the gates of hell shall not prevail against it. And I will give unto thee the keys of the kingdom of heaven: and whatsoever thou shalt bind on earth shall be bound in heaven: and whatsoever thou shalt loose on earth shall be loosed in heaven.‡ (16:18-19)

PARABLES §

Matthew contains twenty-three parables, ten of which have no counterparts in Mark or Luke.

The House on the Rock and the House on the Sand (7:24-27). The Sermon on the Mount ends with an arresting parable. Any man who hears his words, Jesus says, but fails to obey them is like one who builds his house upon the sands, where it will be easily destroyed by winds and floods; but any who hears and

---

* It should be noted that this is a positive statement of a general rule for man's conduct. Some negative versions appear in pre-Christian Judaistic teachings, and both positive and negative versions may be found in the precepts of Lao-tzu (or -tse), Confucius, and Plato. See Johnson and Buttrick, *IB*, VII, 329-330; also *DB*, p. 967. Another Christian version of the Golden Rule appears in Luke 6:31.

† The word *Peter* is here a pun. The Greek for "rock" is *petros* (Aramaic *cephas*). *DB*, p. 972.

‡ Roman Catholics believe that here Jesus is appointing Peter as head of the Church, and they consider the popes as Peter's successors. Protestants, on the other hand, maintain that when Jesus used the word "church" (Greek *ekklesia*), he had in mind no formal religious institution. This passage in Matthew, representing St. Peter as holding the "keys of the kingdom," is probably the origin of the tradition that the Apostle locks and unlocks the gate of heaven.

§ For a list of these parables, see above, p. 12.

obeys is like a man whose house is firmly built on solid rock so as to withstand the buffetings of the elements.

The Backsliding Demoniac (12:43-45). Jesus likens his "wicked generation" to a demoniac who has been cleansed of an unclean spirit but allows seven worse ones to enter him; so also does "this generation" purify itself of one sin but replace it with numerous others.

Six Parables on the New Doctrine (13:24-50). In six parables Jesus attempts to explain to the people the nature of God's Kingdom ° and to indicate to them what will happen to those who either reject or accept his own new teachings. Two parables (The Hidden Treasure and The Pearl of Great Price †) are concerned with the value of devotion to Jesus' doctrines; two others (The Mustard Seed and The Leaven) encourage a small group of believers to spread those doctrines; and the last two (The Tares and The Dragnet) seem to discourage any demands for compromise between good and evil.

The Lost Sheep (18:11-14). Jesus proclaims that God is interested in every individual, just as a shepherd would be concerned over the straying of a single sheep out of a flock of a hundred. "For the Son of man is come to save that which was lost."

The Unmerciful Servant (18:21-35). In answer to questions by Peter, Jesus tells the Disciples that one must be willing to forgive not merely seven times but seventy times seven—that is, indefinitely. To illustrate his point, he tells the Parable of the Unmerciful Servant, who was released from a great debt by his master but refused to cancel a small debt of his own underling. Jesus means that we cannot expect forgiveness from God if we do not forgive others for their offenses to us.

The Laborers in the Vineyard (20:1-16). Jesus tells a story of a number of workers who, though employed for different lengths of time, were all paid alike at the end of the day—much to the displeasure of those who had labored longest. The lesson is that God goes beyond the bounds of justice and deals mercifully

---

° For the meaning of this phrase see note ° on p. 24, above. Matthew uses the phrases "Kingdom of God" and "Kingdom of Heaven" interchangeably.

† George Herbert adapts this parable to his own life in his poem "The Pearl"; and Hawthorne, in *The Scarlet Letter*, has Hester Prynne name her daughter "Pearl" because for her Hester has sacrificed everything, including her reputation.

with his children, being willing to reward all who serve him, even those who are devout only during the latter part of life.

The Two Sons (21:28-32). This story relates that two boys are told by their father to work in the vineyard; one says that he will, but does not; the other says that he will not, but does. The lesson is that service, though performed late and perhaps reluctantly, is preferable to good intentions which are not carried out. Maybe Jesus is saying also that such sinners as tax collectors and harlots may get more reward from God than the orthodox who profess respect for divine commandments but fail to obey them.

The Wedding Feast (22:1-14). When the invited guests fail to attend the celebration of the marriage of a king's son, the king sends his servants to summon the invitees, but the latter murder the servants and do not come to the feast. Then, after destroying the murderers, the king sends servants to offer invitations to everybody they see on the highways. Now many attend, but one comes without a wedding garment and is cast out. The parable is an illustration of the Jews' rejection of the prophets (the servants) and of Jesus (the son), and of the Gentiles' acceptance of Jesus. The man cast out represents those who fail to respond wholeheartedly to Jesus' message. It is possible that Matthew is telling a parable given in an earlier form by Luke (Luke 14:16-24).[33]

Five Parables on Preparedness. After arriving at Jerusalem, Jesus tells the Disciples that his Second Coming may take place at any moment after his death and without any warning. Everybody, therefore, should use his time to the greatest advantage and should live a holy and virtuous life so as always to be ready for this anticipated event. In order to emphasize these points, he tells five parables.

THE HOUSEHOLDER AND THE THIEF (24:42-44). Just as a householder would keep watch against a thief if he knew when the thief was coming, so everybody would be better prepared for Jesus' Second Coming if he knew when to expect it. The godly must be continuously expectant.

THE WISE STEWARD (24:45-51). Everyone should be like a wise and faithful steward left in charge of a household in the absence of the master. On his return the master will reward the steward if he finds that he has been kind to underlings, but will "cut him asunder" if the steward has mistreated them.

THE TEN VIRGINS (25:1-13). The coming of the Kingdom of

Heaven will take many unawares, like five foolish virgins who failed to provide oil for their lamps before the arrival of the bridegroom. Five wise virgins had oil and were able to welcome the bridegroom. While the foolish ones were procuring oil, the bridegroom arrived; and when they knocked at the door, he said, "I know you not."

THE TALENTS * (25:14-30). The Parable of the Talents tells that a certain lord, before setting out on a journey, gave five talents to one servant, two to a second, and one to a third, each according to his ability. Upon the lord's return, the servant with the five talents employed them in trade and gained five more; the servant with two had also doubled his principal; but the servant with only one talent had buried it and so had profited nothing. In wrath the lord took the one talent from the slothful servant and gave it to the servant who had earned five talents. So God expects us to use our talents for his profit.

THE SHEEP AND THE GOATS (25:31-46). Jesus says that when he returns to earth a second time, he will gather all men about him and separate the good from the bad, just as a shepherd separates his sheep from his goats. The good, who have served and obeyed Jesus, will inherit eternal life in God's Kingdom, but the wicked shall receive everlasting punishment. When the righteous ask how they have served Jesus, the answer will be: "Inasmuch as ye have done it unto one of the least of these my brethren, ye have done it unto me" (25:40).

THE TRIAL, THE CRUCIFIXION, AND THE RESURRECTION (CHS. 26–28)

Though still leaning heavily on Mark's narrative, Matthew (perhaps following oral traditions) records several incidents and details pertaining to the events of Passion Week which are not in the earlier Gospel.

Concerning Judas Iscariot's role in the plot against Jesus, where Mark says that the conspirators promise to give Judas "money" (14:11), Matthew is more specific: the plotters offer him "thirty pieces of silver" (26:15). In Mark's account of the Last Supper, Jesus condemns the Disciple who is going to betray him but does

---

* Here, a *talent* (a unit of weight) means a considerable amount of money (perhaps $1,000). The parable has given rise to our use of the word to mean "natural endowment."

not disclose the betrayer's identity (14:21); in Matthew (26:25), however, Judas asks: "Master, is it I?" and Jesus replies: "Thou hast said." After Jesus has been delivered to Pilate, Matthew adds that Judas becomes so conscience-stricken that he returns the silver to the chief priests and then hangs himself. The priests and elders use the money to buy a potters' field for the burial of strangers (27:3-10).

Matthew adds, too, that during the trial of Jesus, Pilate's wife urges her husband to have nothing to do with so righteous a man, for, she says, she has "suffered many things this day in a dream because of him" (27:19). Perhaps influenced by his wife's warning, Pilate performs the famous gesture of hand-washing, symbolic of his desire to disclaim guilt for the conviction of a just person (27:24-25).

Directly after the Crucifixion, according to Matthew there is a great earthquake, and many dead saints emerge from their opened tombs, enter Jerusalem, and appear to many people (27:51-53).

Two other passages peculiar to Matthew's Gospel relate the following: (1) that the chief priests and Pharisees persuade Pilate to set a watch at the Holy Sepulchre lest Jesus' Disciples steal the body and proclaim that their Master has risen from the dead, as he predicted he would do (27:62-66); and (2) that after the Resurrection the chief priests and elders bribe the Roman guards to say that Jesus' body was stolen while those guards were asleep (28:11-15).

Matthew supplies some graphic details concerning the events of the first Easter morning. There is another great earthquake (28:2), and Mark's young man in a white garment sitting within the tomb (16:5) is called "the angel of the Lord" whose countenance is "like lightning, and his raiment white as snow" (28:2-3).

Finally, Matthew omits Jesus' reappearance to the Disciples in Judea (recorded by both Mark and Luke), and, even more surprising, he does not mention the Ascension. He does report (28:16-20) that Jesus appears to the Eleven in Galilee and delivers to them this last missionary appeal: "Go ye therefore, and teach all nations, baptizing them in the name of the Father, and of the Son, and of the Holy Ghost: Teaching them to observe all things whatsoever I have commanded you: and lo, I am with you alway, even unto the end of the world."

4

The Gospel According to Luke: The
Most Poetic and Artistic of the Synoptics

The same eminent critic, Ernest Renan, who called Matthew's Gospel "the most important book ever written," has hailed the Gospel according to Luke as "the most beautiful book there has ever been." [1] It is perhaps also the most beloved book in the world.

It is beloved by all who know it because the author was in himself so lovable, because he was content to lose himself completely in one greater than he, and because he loved men and women with a tenderness which at times is almost heartbreaking in its genuineness." * [2]

AUTHORSHIP, DATE AND PLACE, SOURCES, STYLE

This tender and self-effacing author, Luke, was the "beloved physician" (Col. 4:14) who accompanied St. Paul on several of his missionary journeys. It is refreshing to discover, amidst the welter of scholarly arguments concerning Biblical authorship, that nearly everybody agrees that the third Gospel was written by Luke. The tradition ascribing the book to Luke extends back to the second century, and there is little reason to challenge its accuracy. [3]

There is no such unanimity of opinion, however, about the date and the place of composition. The book was certainly written after the Gospel of Mark, for it uses Mark as one of its main sources. The Gospels of Matthew and Luke were apparently written at about the same time but independently of each other.

---

* Luke is also the author of the Acts of the Apostles, which is a sequel to his Gospel. All the following introduction to the Gospel (relating to authorship, date, style, etc.) applies also to Acts.

Chapter 21 of Luke appears to reflect the fall of Jerusalem (A.D. 70) and Domitian's persecution of the Christians (81–96). The lack of reference to Paul's epistles, on the other hand, indicates that Luke's Gospel was written before 95, by which time the epistles were in general circulation. Whether Luke knew Josephus' history of the Jewish people (written *ca.* 95–96) is an unsettled question. Taking all these matters into consideration, most Biblical scholars agree that about A.D. 90 is the most likely date of composition.[4]

The place of composition has to be left to guesswork.[5] Rome, Ephesus, and Corinth have all been suggested. Ancient tradition associates Luke with Antioch (in Syria), but there is no evidence that he wrote his Gospel there.

Luke himself clearly states one of his purposes in writing the book. The preface (1:1-4) says that inasmuch as many people have written narratives about Jesus *—apparently conflicting ones—Luke has decided to prepare an orderly and trustworthy account for Theophilus (evidently a high Roman official and perhaps a recent convert to Christianity).[6] A second purpose of the third Gospel is to convince the Imperial Roman government that the Christians are not a seditious or subversive sect; Luke emphasizes Pilate's exoneration of Jesus as an innocent and harmless man (23:22) and lays the blame for the Crucifixion principally upon the Jews.[7] A third purpose—really the underlying purpose of the entire Gospel—is to prove to the whole Gentile world that Jesus is the universal Savior, the compassionate Healer and Teacher, who came to demonstrate God's great love for all human beings, to relieve their suffering, and to take away their sins.

The tone, consequently, of Luke's Gospel is that of tenderness and sympathy. It has "an appealing emotional quality, a feeling for values of the heart."[8] It is the Gospel of "the poor and outcast, . . . of tolerance, . . . of prayer, . . . of joy, . . . of the home."[9] Women play a far larger role in this Gospel than in any other.

Luke's preface states that he is writing his own recollection of events, but he undoubtedly took considerable pains to gather as

---

* This portion of the preface is highly significant, for it indicates the circulation of numerous no-longer-existent Gospels in the first century A.D.

much information as he could and to authenticate it to the best
of his ability. This information appears to have been derived
from four main sources: (1) St. Mark's Gospel. Luke uses about
60 per cent of Mark's 661 verses; these contribute the basis for
about a third of Luke's total of 1148 verses.[10] Luke, then, omits
more of Mark than Matthew does; but where he uses the first
Gospel, he follows the Marcan order almost exactly (with two
exceptions); Luke is "the joy of the harmonist, just as Matthew
is his despair." [11] Luke uses six major blocks of Marcan material
and several minor ones; he omits Mark 6:45–8:26 (the "Great
Omission").[12] His chief reasons for departing from Mark are (a)
to improve on Mark's style, (b) to omit irrelevancies, (c) to
soften or idealize the pictures of Jesus and the Disciples, (d) to
omit incongruous or incomprehensible incidents (for example,
the cursing of the fig tree in Mark 11:12-14, 20-22), and (e) to
utilize other sources of information which he considered important.[13] In one place Luke "seriously confuses" the course of the
story by inserting a long passage (9:51–18:14, the "Travel Document") into the Marcan narrative. The insertion gives the impression that Jesus went slowly from Galilee to Jerusalem—that a
large portion of his ministry was spent on this journey. Luke's
reason for so placing this passage was probably that when he
had followed Mark's story to the point where Jesus was to leave
Galilee, he discovered that he still had a great deal of valuable
unused material which obviously pertained to some undetermined
period in Jesus' life before the arrival in Jerusalem.[14] (2) The
Q document. About a fifth of Luke's book is derived from Q; [15]
this consists (as in Matthew) of sayings of Jesus. (3) The L
source. A source used only by Luke and known to us only by its
inclusion in his Gospel is now designated as "L." It is believed to
be of Palestinian provenance and to have provided Luke (a) with
the material found in the "Travel Document" and (b) with the
non-Marcan portions of the Passion and post-Resurrection narrative (22:14-24, passim).[16] Nearly 40 per cent of Luke is derived
from L.[17] (4) Oral tradition. The birth and infancy narratives
and the hymns in the first two chapters are believed to have
been derived from oral tradition. The hymns were perhaps used
in the church services in Jerusalem and were probably originally
written in either Hebrew or Aramaic.[18]

Luke was a skillful writer. His language is fluent, graceful, polished, nonliterary Greek (*Koiné*); his vocabulary is large, and his choice of words is exact. He replaces Mark's stringy co-ordinate clauses with balanced and periodic constructions. He is careful to observe the rules of Greek grammar and syntax. He excels in descriptions of scenes (the Nativity, 2:6-14), in vivid portraiture (Simeon, 2:25; Anna, 2:37; Peter, James, and John, with sleep-heavy eyes, 9:32), and in narrative power (the parables of the Good Samaritan, 10:30-37, and the Prodigal Son, 15:11-32). He has a strong dramatic sense and makes much use of psychological contrast (the Pharisee vs. the sinful woman, 7:36-48; the Samaritan vs. the priest and the Levite, 10:30-37; Mary vs. Martha, 10:38-42). Possessing a keen appreciation of poetry, he preserves for us the earliest Christian hymns (the Magnificat, 1:46-55; the Benedictus, 1:68-79; the Gloria in Excelsis, 2:14; and the Nunc Dimittis, 2:29-32). A graceful poetic charm pervades the whole Gospel.[19] These merits distinguish Luke as the greatest literary artist of the New Testament.

The organization of material in this Gospel is similar to that in Mark: introduction (birth of John the Baptist and birth and childhood of Jesus), Chs. 1–2; baptism and temptation of Jesus, 3:1–4:13; ministry in Galilee 4:14–9:50; ministry in Perea, 9:51–19:28; ministry in Judea, 19:28–22:38; arrest, trials, Crucifixion, Resurrection, and Ascension, 22:39–24:53.

BIRTH OF JOHN THE BAPTIST (1:5-25, 39-45, 57-80)

After a brief preface addressed to Theophilus, Luke begins his Gospel with the story of the birth of John the Baptist:

During the reign of Herod the Great the angel Gabriel appears to Zacharias (R.S.V.: Zechariah), a good and upright priest, and tells him that his barren wife Elisabeth is going to bear a son.* This child will be filled with the Holy Spirit even while he is unborn; God will "go before him in the spirit and power" of Elijah † so that he will lead many Israelites back to God and prepare them "for the Lord" (1:17). Zacharias' son (like the ancient Nazarites when they vowed consecration to God) will drink no alcoholic beverages. Like his ancestor Abraham, Zacharias doubts the angel's prophecy, for both he and Elisabeth are "well stricken

---

* See footnote * on p. 18, above.

† It should be remembered that many people believed John the Baptist to be a reincarnation of Elijah. See John 1:25.

in years." In order to punish him for his skepticism and also to furnish him with a "sign" of the validity of the prediction, Gabriel strikes Zacharias with dumbness, which is to continue until the birth of the son.[20] Elisabeth conceives, as the angel has foretold.

Six months later, when Mary, the wife of Joseph and the cousin of Elisabeth, comes for a visit, at Mary's greeting the babe in Elisabeth's womb leaps for joy—apparently aware that Mary is going to become the mother of the Messiah. Elisabeth blesses Mary and rejoices with her over the prospect of Jesus' birth.

When Elisabeth, though "well stricken with years," gives birth to a son, her friends urge that he be named for his father, but Elisabeth insists on the name "John" (meaning "God is gracious"). Zacharias (whose punishment for incredulity includes deafness as well as dumbness, for the people have to communicate with him by signs) writes, "His name is John." Immediately the curse is removed from Zacharias, and he prophesies, in phrases reminiscent of the Old Testament, praising God for keeping his Covenant with the Israelites and for sending John as a forerunner of the Messiah (the famous Benedictus, 1:68-79).

John grows into manhood and takes up his abode in the wilderness until the time is ripe for his revelations to the Israelites.

THE GENEALOGY, THE BIRTH, AND THE CHILDHOOD OF JESUS

Luke gives us the most nearly complete account of the ancestry and early years of Jesus.

Genealogy (3:23-38). Luke's genealogy of Jesus differs in several respects from that given by Matthew. First, many of the ancestors are different. Luke gives Heli instead of Jacob as the father of Joseph (the husband of Mary) and traces the ancestry from Nathan instead of from David's son Solomon. Second, and perhaps more important, Luke traces the ancestry not only back to Abraham but all the way back to Adam; the inference is that Luke is interested in showing that Jesus is not merely the Messiah descended from David and promised by the prophets as a liberator of the Jews, but also the universal Christ.

The Annunciation and the Magnificat (1:26-38, 46-55). A short while before Mary's visit to Elisabeth, the angel Gabriel appears to Mary and addresses her: "Hail, thou that art highly fa-

voured, the Lord is with thee: blessed art thou among women." *
Mary is troubled, but Gabriel assures her that there is nothing to
fear. She will conceive, he says, and will bear a son, whom she is
to name Jesus.

He shall be great, and shall be called the Son of the Highest; and the
Lord God shall give unto him the throne of his father David: and he
shall reign over the house of Jacob for ever; and of his kingdom there
shall be no end. (1:32-33)

(These words announce the fulfillment of the prophecies in II
Samuel 7:13-16 and Isaiah 9:6-7.[21]) Amazed, Mary says that she
is still a virgin. Gabriel replies that the Holy Spirit will beget the
child:

The Holy Ghost shall come upon thee, and the power of the Highest
shall overshadow thee: therefore also that holy thing which shall be
born of thee shall be called the Son of God. (1:35)

After informing her of the conception of John the Baptist, Gabriel
departs.

In haste Mary goes to see Elisabeth. As soon as she has been
congratulated by her cousin, Mary pours forth her praise to God
for his goodness to her and to her nation in the famous Magnificat
("My soul doth magnify the Lord," 1:46-55).[22]

Birth and Infancy of Jesus † (2:1-40). Luke alone among the
Gospel writers tells us the beautiful story of Christ's birth in the
manger:

Caesar Augustus decreed that everyone in the Roman Empire
must return to his family's native city in order to be enrolled for
purposes of taxation. Consequently, Joseph (of the lineage of

---

* This salutation became in the Latin version the "Ave Maria," afterward
the title and opening words of many hymns addressed to the Virgin Mary.
The music for some of the best-known versions has been composed by Bach
(rearranged by Gounod), Kahn, Schipa, Schubert, and Verdi.

† The study of comparative religion reveals various stories about mytho-
logical or legendary births which in one way or another are similar to Luke's
account of Christ's Nativity: the Egyptian myth of Osiris, the Roman legend
of the shepherds' caring for Romulus and Remus, and the Iranian tale of the
shepherds' keeping watch over the birth of Mithra. (See Gilmour, *IB*, VIII,
48.)

David) goes from Nazareth to Bethlehem. With him is Mary, who by this time is "great with child." Upon arrival in the small town, the couple discover that all the rooms in the inn * are already taken; for this reason they are forced to lodge in a manger. There Mary gives birth to Jesus and wraps him in swaddling clothes (2:7).

On the nearby hillsides while some shepherds are guarding their flocks at night, an angel appears before them, and the shepherds are frightened. The angel reassures them:

Fear not: for, behold, I bring you good tidings of great joy, which shall be to all people. For unto you is born this day in the city of David a Saviour, which is Christ the Lord. (2:10-11)

The shepherds will find the babe in a manger in Bethlehem, the angel says. Suddenly there is with the angel a multitude of the "heavenly host," praising God and saying, "Glory to God in the highest, and on earth peace, good will toward men" (2:14).†

Following the angel's directions, the shepherds come to the holy manger, offer praises to God, and spread abroad the good news.

When Jesus is eight days old, he is circumcised in accordance with Jewish custom, and about a month later he is brought to the Temple in Jerusalem to be presented to the Lord.‡

Dwelling in Jerusalem at the time is a devout old man named Simeon, who has been promised by the Holy Spirit that he will live to see the Messiah. He sees the baby Jesus in the Temple and recognizes him as the Christ. Taking the child in his arms, he utters the prayer (now well known as the "Nunc Dimittis"):

* "Inn" may be an inaccurate translation; perhaps "living room" would be better. The Greek word usually referred to the main room of a peasant house; the "manger" or "stable" was the space on the ground on each side of the steps mounting to the living room. Animals were fed and sheltered in the mangers, especially in inclement weather. (See Findlay, *ABC*, p. 1034.)

† This is, of course, the now-familiar "Gloria in Excelsis Deo." The last part of the verse, according to other manuscripts (followed by the Revised Standard Version), reads "peace among men with whom he is pleased" (see Gilmour, *IB*, VIII, 55).

‡ This conflicts with the account given in Matt. 2:13-23, which tells us that the Holy Family went to Egypt and remained there till the death of Herod. Such a journey alone, without any sojourn in Egypt, would have required far longer than forty days. (See *DB*, p. 964.)

Lord, now lettest thou thy servant depart in peace, according to thy word: For mine eyes have seen thy salvation, Which thou has prepared before the face of all people; A light to lighten the Gentiles, and the glory of thy people Israel. (2:29-32)

Likewise, the aged prophetess Anna sees the baby, gives thanks to God, and recommends the child to all who are waiting for the Messiah.

Soon afterward Mary and Joseph return with their son to Nazareth.

The Boy Jesus in the Temple (2:41-52). It is Luke alone who records the one incident in the canonical Scriptures * concerning the boyhood of Jesus. When he is twelve years old, he accompanies his parents to Jerusalem for the Passover festival. When Joseph and Mary begin the journey back to Nazareth, Jesus remains in Jerusalem. Noting his absence after the first day, his parents return to Jerusalem, where they discover him in the Temple, "sitting in the midst of the doctors, both hearing them, and asking them questions." The bystanders and the learned teachers alike are amazed at his understanding and knowledge. His parents rebuke him for causing them anxiety and requiring them to search for him. He replies that they should have known that he would be engaged in his "Father's business" (2:49).

"And Jesus increased in wisdom and stature, and in favour with God and man" (2:52).†

MIRACLES

Luke relates twenty miracles; fifteen of these appear also in either Matthew or Mark, or both, and have already been discussed. One (the Draught of Fishes) is told only by Luke and John.

According to Luke (5:1-11), very early in his ministry Jesus asks Simon to take him in his boat a short distance from shore so that he may preach to the people from the boat. Afterward he tells Simon to go farther out to sea and to cast his nets. Simon replies that he has fished all night and caught nothing, but that he will try once more. Now the catch is so great that the nets

* The apocryphal Gospel of Thomas depicts Jesus as an ostentatious "boy wonder" (Gilmour, *IB*, VIII, 66).

† Compare the statement about the boy Samuel in I Sam. 2:26.

break. Simon's partners, James and John, bring another boat to help, and both boats nearly sink with the huge loads of fish. Awed by the miracle, Simon falls before Jesus, confesses that he is a sinful man and, frightened, begs Jesus to depart. Jesus tells Simon not to be afraid but to follow him and he will catch men instead of fish. The fishermen forsake their occupation and follow Jesus.*

The four miracles that are recorded only by Luke are the revival of the dead son of a widow in the town of Nain (7:11-17), the curing of a crippled woman (13:10-17), the curing of a man with dropsy (14:1-6), and the healing of ten lepers (17:11-19).

PARABLES

Of the four Evangelists, Luke is perhaps the best reteller of parables. He preserves for us thirty of them, of which the following sixteen are peculiar to his Gospel.†

The Two Debtors (7:36-50). When censured by a Pharisee for associating with a sinful woman, Jesus tells the story of the Two Debtors. One owed a creditor five hundred denarii and the other owed fifty; the creditor canceled both debts. Jesus asks Simon, the Pharisee, which of the debtors loved the creditor more. Simon answers, the one who was "forgiven" the larger debt. Jesus agrees and says that likewise the woman whose sins he has forgiven loves him more than does Simon, whose sins are few.

The Good Samaritan (10:25-37). One of the most beloved of all Jesus' parables is that about the Good Samaritan.‡ After Jesus has told a lawyer § that the two greatest commandments are to love God and to love one's neighbor, the lawyer asks: "And who is my neighbour?" Jesus answers him with a story about a man who, en route from Jerusalem to Jericho, was attacked by robbers,

---

* Compare Mark's version of the calling, 1:16-20. Unlike Mark, Luke does not mention here the calling of Andrew.

† See above, p. 12, the table of Christ's parables as they appear in all three Synoptic Gospels.

‡ The point of the story is enhanced by the fact that for four centuries the Jews had loathed the Samaritans for what the Jews considered collaboration with the enemy (the Assyrians and the Babylonians) and for defiling the Israelitish blood by intermarriage with foreigners.

§ Luke uses the word *lawyer;* Mark (12:28) calls the questioner a scribe.

stripped of his clothing, and left half dead on the roadside. First a priest and then a Levite (both supposedly religious and merciful men) saw the victim, but passed by on the other side of the road. Next a Samaritan came along, dressed the man's wounds, took him to an inn, and paid the innkeeper to care for him. Jesus asks the lawyer which of the three passers-by was a neighbor to the wounded man. When the lawyer nominates the Samaritan, Jesus says: "Go, and do thou likewise." In this way the Master teaches that love "must know no limits of race and ask no enquiry. Who needs me is my neighbour. Whom at the given time and place I can help with my active love, he is my neighbor, and I am his." [23]

The Importunate Friend (11:5-10). A parable with a touch of humor illustrates God's willingness to help human beings when they ask his aid. Jesus says (in effect) to the Disciples: Suppose you were to knock on your friend's door at midnight and ask him to lend you some bread. At first the friend might refuse out of annoyance at being disturbed at such an hour. But if you should continue knocking, the friend would give you the bread merely for the sake of getting rid of you. God, even more than human friends, will listen to your persistent petitions: "Ask, and it shall be given you; seek, and ye shall find; knock, and it shall be opened unto you."

The Rich Fool (12:16-21). In order to illustrate the folly of putting one's trust in possessions, Jesus tells a tale about a rich man whose land produced so plentifully that he decided to pull down his barns and build bigger ones for the storage of his crops. The man thought to himself:

I will say to my soul, Soul, thou has much goods laid up for many years; take thine ease, eat, drink, and be merry. But God said unto him, Thou fool, this night thy soul shall be required of thee: then whose shall those things be, which thou has provided? (12:19-20)

The Barren Fig Tree (13:6-9).[24] Urging every man to be diligent and productive,* Jesus tells about a fig tree which for three years has borne no fruit. The owner commands his servant to

---

* Compare the parables of the Talents (Matt. 25:14-30) and the Pounds (Luke 19:11-17).

cut it down, but the servant asks his master to spare it one more year; he will dig around it and fertilize it, and if it still bears no fruit, it will be destroyed.

The Impolite Wedding Guest (14:7-11). Jesus repeatedly preaches against personal pride. A parable (told at the house of a Pharisee and thus probably aimed principally at the Pharisees) warns against such things as scrambling for seats of honor at a wedding feast. The parable, using second-person address, says: If you are a wedding guest, do not seat yourself in the place of honor, for your host may ask you to give up your place to someone of greater importance, and you will be shamed before all the guests; but take the lowest place, and then your host may invite you to move to a higher place, and you will gain the respect of all. "For whosoever exalteth himself shall be abased; and he that humbleth himself shall be exalted." Jesus perhaps intends for the warning to apply to those who are guilty of all sorts of self-exaltation.* [25]

The Banquet (14:16-24). Luke's Parable of the Banquet is a variant of Matthew's Parable of the Wedding Feast (22:1-10), but the details and the implications are so different that some commentators list the stories as different parables. In Luke the host is just "a certain man," not a king as in Matthew; the meal is simply "a great supper," not a wedding feast; there is only one servant (probably not intended to represent Christ; [26] and instead of murdering the servant, the invitees merely offer excuses for their unwillingness to attend the banquet. Luke, of course, says nothing of the invitees and their city, since in his version the host is not a king and the invitees do nothing to deserve death.

Counting the Cost: Twin Parables Concerning Discipleship (14:28-33). In twin parables Jesus teaches that the burdens of discipleship are heavy and must not be assumed without consideration of the sacrifices involved. To do so, he says, would be (a) like beginning the building of a tower without first counting the cost and deciding whether one had enough money to pay for its completion, or (b) like a king's preparing for war without calculating the strength of the enemy. Such short-sighted undertakings will lead to disaster. A disciple must be willing to forsake everything that he has.

* Compare the advice to James, John, and others in Matt. 20:26-27 and 23:12.

The Lost Coin (15:8-10). Similar to the Parable of the Lost Sheep (which Luke tells in 15:1-7) is that of the Lost Coin. If a woman were to lose one of ten silver coins, she would search diligently until she found it and then call in her neighbors to rejoice with her over the recovery. In the same way, God rejoices over the repentance and rehabilitation of one sinner.

The Prodigal Son (15:11-32). Probably no other parable has been so frequently cited as that of the Prodigal Son. The parable concerns a man and his two sons. The younger boy asks for his inheritance, receives it, and soon spends it in profligate living. Poverty-stricken and remorseful, he decides to return home and to offer to work as a servant, being unworthy of acceptance as a son. But the father welcomes him joyfully and orders the servants to bring him a robe, a ring, and shoes and to kill "the fatted calf" for a feast. The elder son, who has always been obedient and dutiful, resents the celebration for his younger brother; his father has never provided a feast for *him*. The father rebukes him mildly: "Son, thou art ever with me, and all that I have is thine. It was meet that we should make merry, and be glad: for this thy brother was dead, and is alive again; and was lost, and is found" (15:31-32).

Unlike most of the other parables, which have only one main point to convey, this story teaches two lessons: first, that God (here represented by the father) is a loving, merciful, and generous God who is eager to forgive the repentant sinner (the younger son) and to rejoice over his reformation; * and second, that the righteous man (the elder son) should share God's readiness to forgive and to love.

The Dishonest Steward (16:1-9). The Parable of the Dishonest Steward is a strange story: A rich man decides to dismiss his steward for wasteful management of the estate. Before the dismissal has been put into effect, the steward tries to curry favor with his master's debtors by dishonestly allowing them to reduce their bills of indebtedness—hoping that they will support him when he is jobless. The master discovers the dishonest acts of the steward, but he commends him for his shrewdness! Jesus comments: "For the children of this world are in their generation wiser than the children of light" (16:8)—that is, schemers seem

---

* Compare the parables of the Lost Sheep and the Lost Coin.

to be more practical than saints. And, Jesus adds: "Make to yourselves friends of the mammon [money] of unrighteousness; that,
when ye fail, they may receive you into everlasting habitations"
(16:9). The interpretation of this advice is difficult. Is Jesus saying that, since all money is evil, we should make wise use of it by
doing such things as giving to the poor, so that we shall have
an "everlasting habitation" in heaven?* [27] Or is he being sarcastic,
urging us ironically to make friends of the rich so that we may rely
on them when everything else fails us? [28]

The Rich Man † and Lazarus (16:19-31). A miserable beggar
named Lazarus lies at the gate of a rich man, who enjoys all the
pleasures of this world. Lazarus dies and goes to dwell in "Abraham's bosom." The rich man also dies, but he goes to hell. He
cries out to Abraham to send Lazarus with a drop of water to
cool his tongue. Abraham replies that the rich man had his enjoy-
ment on earth and, besides, the gulf between heaven and hell is
impassable. The rich man then asks that Lazarus be sent to earth
to warn the rich man's brothers about the tortures of hell. Abraham denies this request also, for the brothers have been warned
by Moses and the prophets; and if that warning does not convince them, nothing will—not even one risen from the dead.

Some commentators have considered this parable an attack on
the wealthy Sadducees (represented by the rich man) for their
materialism and for their refusal to believe in the afterlife (here
Lazarus would represent Christ himself, and Jesus would be pre-
dicting their denial of his Resurrection). But perhaps Jesus is
simply saying, as is his wont, that the first shall be last and the
last first, that the poor will be rewarded in heaven, and that men
stubbornly refuse to obey the Law and the prophets. Perhaps he
means to imply that the rich will be punished for their neglect
of the needy.[29]

The Farmer and His Servant (17:7-10). This short parable
emphasizes the point that if we merely do our *duty*, we are un-
profitable servants of God and deserve no reward. Jesus asks

---

* Compare Matthew's passage about laying up treasures in heaven (6:19-
20).

† The Latin word for "rich" was *dives;* hence the word is often used as
if it were the name of the character. The parable is the only passage in the
Gospels which gives us a picture of the regions of punishment and reward
after death. (Gilmour, *IB*, VIII, 290.)

the Disciples (in effect): Would any of you call in a servant (i.e., slave) from plowing or feeding cattle and urge him to eat before he had prepared the meal for you? And would you thank him for doing what you had commanded? No. Neither should you expect any special reward from God for obeying his commands.

The Persistent Widow and the Unjust Judge (18:1-8). This story is similar to the one about the Importunate Friend. A wicked judge who neither fears God nor regards man refuses for a long time to help a poor widow who seeks vengeance against her enemy. The widow, however, is so persistent that the judge finally aids her so that she will stop annoying him. If the judge, acting from such unworthy motives, will listen to the widow's entreaties, how much more readily will God avenge "his own elect"?

The parable has apparently gone through several stages of transmission which illustrate what may have happened to much of the Gospel material: a simple parable (vss. 2-5) recommending persistence in prayer, an added injunction to Christians to pray for a speedy Day of Judgment (vss. 6-8a), and a second addition (v. 8b) alluding to divisions and heresies in the Church.[30]

The Pharisee and the Publican (18:9-14). As an attack on pride and self-righteousness (such as that of some of the Pharisees), Jesus tells this story: A Pharisee and a publican (tax collector) go simultaneously into the Temple to pray. The Pharisee thanks God that he is better than other men: he commits no sins, and he goes beyond the requirements of the Law in fasting and tithing. In contrast, the publican, aware of his own unworthiness, beats his breast and prays contritely: "God be merciful to me a sinner." Jesus declares that it is the publican rather than the Pharisee who goes home "justified" (that is, acceptable to God).

THE DISCIPLESHIP OF WOMEN

Luke more than any of the other Evangelists shows sympathy for women and interest in their physical, economic, and religious welfare.[31] It is his Gospel alone that contains the parables of the Persistent Widow and the woman's Lost Coin, and also the accounts of Elisabeth, the Virgin Mary, the old prophetess Anna, the widow of Nain, the women who minister to Jesus in Galilee, Mary and Martha and their different ways of showing love for

Jesus,* and the women who follow Jesus to the Crucifixion. Three of Luke's stories about women deserve special attention here.

Jesus and the Sinful Woman (7:36-50). Once when Jesus is dining at the home of Simon, the Pharisee, a disreputable woman bathes his feet with her tears of penitence, dries them with her hair, kisses them, and then anoints them with an ointment brought in an alabaster box. Simon silently accuses Jesus of being no prophet: a real prophet, he thinks, would have discerned the nature of the woman and spurned her. Reading his thoughts, Jesus tells Simon the Parable of the Two Debtors. He remarks that the woman's love for him must be far greater than Simon's own, for where Simon has provided no water for a footbath, no oil for the head, and no kiss, the penitent woman has given his feet a bath of tears and dried them with the hair of her head; she has anointed them with precious ointment and has kissed them many times. Then Jesus forgives the woman's sins—to the shocked disapproval of the other guests, who consider him blasphemous for professing to forgive sins.†

The Ministering Women in Galilee (8:1-3). Apparently Jesus and the Twelve are supported not only by "chance hospitality" but also by the contributions of well-to-do women whom Jesus has benefited physically, mentally, or spiritually.[32] Luke introduces three of these women in Chapter 8. One is Mary Magdalene (Mary of Magdala), from whom he has driven seven evil spirits.‡

---

* The Gospel of John (11:1-46, 12:1-8) tells another story about these two sisters of Bethany.

† Told more briefly in Mark 14:3-9. John (12:3) identifies the woman (but does not call her a sinner) with Mary of Bethany, sister of Martha.

‡ Some commentators identify Mary Magdalene with the "sinful woman" of the preceding chapter, but according to Gilmour (*IB*, VIII, 146), there is no reason for this identification. Medieval tradition, nevertheless, regarded Mary Magdalene as a penitent prostitute, and Renaissance paintings and poetry (for example, Crashaw's "Saint Mary Magdalene, or the Weeper") depict her in tears (hence our adjective *maudlin*, a British corruption of Magdalene). None of the Gospels, however, mentions her as particularly sinful; only John (20:11-15) says anything about her weeping. Mark, Matthew, and John all record that she was present at the Crucifixion and at Christ's tomb on the morning of the Resurrection (Mark 15:40-41 and 16:1-9; Matthew 27:56 and 28:1-10; and John 19:25 and 20:1-18). Luke (23:49 and 55) refers to women from Galilee but does not mention Mary specifically as watching the Crucifixion; he does, however, name her as one of those at the scene of the Resurrection (24:10).

Another is Joanna, a woman of wealth and influence, for her husband is the steward of Herod Antipas.* The third is named Susanna.† Luke says that these three "ministered unto him of their substance."

Mary and Martha (10:38-42). In "a certain village" ‡ Jesus visits the home of two sisters named Mary and Martha. Mary sits at Jesus' feet and listens to his teaching, while Martha busies herself with the preparation of an elaborate meal ("much serving"). Martha chides her sister and asks Jesus to command Mary to do her share of the work. But Jesus sides with Mary, who, he says, has "chosen that good part" (listening to his teachings and demonstrating her love for him), whereas Martha has been far too preoccupied with "many things"—material things—to benefit from the golden opportunity for instruction and worship.

TRIAL BEFORE HEROD ANTIPAS (23:6-12)

Though varying only slightly in most places from Mark's and Matthew's accounts of the arrest and trials of Jesus, Luke's version adds one significant incident. When Pilate learns that Jesus is a Galilean, he finds this a sufficient excuse for transferring the prisoner to the jurisdiction of Herod Antipas, who happens to be in Jerusalem at the time. Herod is delighted, because for a long time he has wanted to see one of Jesus' miracles. As in the other accounts of the Master's trials, the chief priests and the scribes accuse him "vehemently" and Jesus refuses to answer any questions. Herod and his soldiers mock him, clothe him in a gorgeous robe, and send him back to Pilate.

SOME INCIDENTS AT THE CRUCIFIXION (23:34, 39-43)

Luke, as we have its text, adds several illuminating details to Mark's story of the Crucifixion.

One such addition (which is not found in any of the early manuscripts of the Gospel, and which may have been a scribe's interpolation) is Christ's praying for those who have crucified him: "Father, forgive them; for they know not what they do." The

---

* Joanna followed Jesus to Jerusalem and was with Mary Magdalene at the discovery of Christ's empty tomb (Luke 24:10).

† Luke's reference (8:3) furnishes all that is known of Susanna.

‡ John (11:1 and 12:1-3) says the village is Bethany and Mary and Martha have a brother named Lazarus, whom Luke does not mention.

antecedent of the pronoun *them* is ambiguous; there is no way of knowing whether it refers to the Jews who have brought about his conviction or the Roman soldiers who have carried out the sentence.[33]

Another addition is concerned with the two "malefactors" who are crucified with Jesus. Whereas Mark mentions them only briefly (15:27-28), Luke reports a conversation which takes place on the crosses. One of the criminals rails at Jesus and scoffingly asks why he does not save himself and them. The other rebukes his fellow. Only Jesus, he says, is being crucified unjustly. Then he says: "Lord, remember me when thou comest into thy kingdom." Jesus accepts this prayer as penitence and promises: "To day shalt thou be with me in paradise."

THE WALK TO EMMAUS (24:13-35)

Only Luke tells the story of the risen Jesus' appearance to two of his former followers on the road to Emmaus, a small town near Jerusalem. While the two men are walking along the road, discussing the Crucifixion and what they have heard concerning the Resurrection, Jesus himself approaches and asks why they seem so sad. In surprise they inquire whether he is unaware of the tragic things which have happened in Jerusalem. When he asks, "What things?" they summarize briefly for him the trials, the Crucifixion, and the rumors of the Resurrection. Jesus rebukes them for not understanding that all those events had been predicted by the prophets and that the Christ had to suffer before he should enter into his glory; then he expounds to them the passages of Scripture concerning the Messiah. As the travelers draw near to Emmaus, Jesus accepts an invitation to spend the evening with them. At dinner he breaks bread and blesses it. Immediately their eyes are "opened" so that they recognize him; then he vanishes. Although it is now late, they rush back to Jerusalem with their news and report it to the Disciples and other followers of Jesus.

THE RISEN JESUS AND THE ASCENSION (24:36-53)

No longer relying on Mark, Luke tells a different story of Jesus' reappearance in Jerusalem and of his Ascension.

While the two travelers are still telling the Jerusalem group about their experiences near and in Emmaus, Christ appears in their midst. The members of the group are terrified, thinking "they had seen a spirit." Jesus assures them that he is not a spirit but is present in the flesh; he eats a piece of fish and some honeycomb [34] to prove his corporeality. As in the other Gospels, he gives them their missionary injunction, walks with them to Bethany, and is then "carried up into heaven." His followers joyfully return to Jerusalem, where they continually worship and praise God in the Temple.

5

The Acts of the Apostles: The Earliest History of the Spread of Christianity

The book of Acts is one of the most valuable historical documents in the Bible. It is the only extant history of the Christian Church written before the third century; without it we should have virtually no record of the growth of Christianity in Palestine or of its spread to Syria, Asia Minor, Greece, and Rome. It is our chief source of information about the life and missionary activities of St. Paul and consequently provides an indispensable biographical and historical background for the understanding of the Pauline epistles.

AUTHORSHIP, SOURCES, DATE, AND PLACE

Although there was a time when some scholars questioned Lucan authorship, now practically everyone ascribes this important book to Luke, the "beloved physician" and the companion of Paul.[1] Both internal and external evidence—style, references to Paul and others, and the testimony of several ancient writers— point to Luke as the author. The book is manifestly a sequel to the third Gospel: both works are addressed to Theophilus, and Acts opens with a reference to "the former treatise [which I have] made," plus a review of some of the events recorded in Luke 24. Scholars believe that the Gospel filled one scroll and Acts a second.

Luke apparently relied on oral sources for most of the first half of Acts. It seems likely that he went about Palestine and Syria gathering what data he could from Jesus' loyal followers— Peter, John, and many lesser ones. Much of the latter part of the book (beginning with Chapter 13) sounds like an eyewitness

account; one should notice especially the four famou[s] passages (16:10-17, 20:5-15, 21:1-18, and 27:1—28:16[)]
the use of the first person plural implies that the aut[hor]
ticipant in the events recounted. Most scholars are in[clined to]
believe that Luke kept a diary or travel journal, that the journal
furnished the data for many portions of Acts, and that the "we"
passages are verbatim excerpts from the journal.[2]

Assumptions as to the date and place of composition of Luke's
Gospel (see pp. 50–52) apply also to Acts. It should be noted that
Acts especially gives evidence of being enlarged and reworked,
perhaps over several decades. When the two-volume Luke-Acts
was finished and despatched to Theophilus is unknown. The
period from A.D. 85 to A.D. 95 seems a likely one.[3]

PURPOSES AND CRITICAL EVALUATION

One commentator [4] has suggested that this work should be
entitled not "Acts of the Apostles" but "Acts of the Holy Spirit."
Its main purpose is to show how the Holy Spirit, working through
Christ's followers, spread the "good news" of Jesus' life and
teaching throughout the Greco-Roman world. According to the
Gospels, Jesus had appointed his Disciples to be missionaries to
all the world and had promised to send the Holy Spirit to aid
and comfort them. The Acts of the Apostles is an account of the
fulfillment of both Jesus' promise and the Disciples' missions.

A secondary purpose, like that of Luke's Gospel, is to defend
Christianity as a nonseditious and benevolent religion. Luke takes
pains to point out that Paul was found innocent every time he
was tried before the Roman authorities. Perhaps the existence of
the second purpose explains why Luke ends the history before
Paul's execution (ca. A.D. 63 or 64).

Some critics have disparaged the historical accuracy of Acts.
They claim that, as a propagandistic narrative, it is colored by
Luke's prejudices and invalidated by his exaggerations. Luke,
they say, naïvely accepts unverifiable stories of miracles, and his
accounts of events differ from Paul's in several details. Furthermore, according to these critics, the speeches attributed to Peter,
Stephen, and Paul must be, in fact, Luke's own oratory, for there
was no stenographer to take down the exact words of those
speakers.

In evaluating such criticisms, one should bear in mind several pertinent considerations. In the first place, Luke employed the techniques and conventions of his age; to accuse him of bias, exaggeration, and credulity is to judge him by modern standards of historiography. He compares favorably with Herodotus, Xenophon, Josephus, Livy, and Tacitus as an accurate reporter in such matters as customs, geography, and topography, which can be verified by historical and archaeological research, Acts has been found to be unusually trustworthy. As for the speeches, it was conventional for a Greek historian to use his own words for the reproduction of an orator's address; Thucydides' "Funeral Oration of Pericles" is a notable example. In the second place, Luke was writing—perhaps sometimes from memory—several decades after the events recorded. It would have been a miracle if his and Paul's accounts had been identical. (Luke was not familiar with Paul's epistles.) In the third place, a comparison of Luke's Acts with the apocryphal "Acts" of various church figures written in the second century A.D. reveals that the latter are romances, whereas Luke's volume is serious history.[5]

STYLE

The Acts of the Apostles ranks high as a work of literature. It has much of the same radiance, warmth, tenderness, and enthusiasm which we have found to be characteristic of Luke's Gospel. The author shows superb skill in presenting dramatic episodes: the events at the time of Pentecost (2:1-41), Philip's running to the chariot of the Ethiopian eunuch (8:26-39), Paul's conversion (9:1-9), and Paul's shipwreck (27:14-44). There are, furthermore, many striking portraits of interesting people: the bold and confident Peter, the shrewd and opportunistic Simon Magus, the deceitful Ananias, and the learned and zealous Paul. The narrative moves smoothly and logically according to a preconceived plan: the tracing of the Gospel farther and farther from Jerusalem.

Luke's dramatic, descriptive, and narrative abilities so impressed Ernest Renan that he labeled the Acts "a new Homer." [6]

CONTENTS

Acts is not a comprehensive history of the whole Christian movement during the first century. It covers only three decades,

from about 33 to about 63; * and it is principally concerned with
the deeds of only two of the Apostles: Peter and Paul. Approxi-
mately half the book is devoted to Paul, about a third to Peter,
and about a sixth to some other Christian leaders.

The contents fall into six distinct parts: (1) the founding of
the Church in Jerusalem (1:1–6:7); (2) the dispersal of the
Christians over Palestine following the martyrdom of Stephen
(6:8–9:31); (3) the spread of the Church in Palestine and Syria
(9:32–12:25); (4) Paul's first missionary journey to Cyprus and
Asia Minor and his return to Jerusalem (13:1–16:5); (5) Paul's
journeys to Macedonia and Greece (16:6–21:14); and (6) the
opposition to Paul, and his journey to Rome (21:15–28:31).[7]

Although this arrangement of material is neatly chronological,
it is perhaps not the most convenient for literary analysis.
Throughout Luke's thirty-year drama several major figures appear on the stage at various times. Let us single out the five most
important characters, gather up the scattered passages pertaining
to each, and consider one by one the five groups of passages.
Our principal *dramatis personae* will be Peter, Stephen, Philip,
Barnabas, and Paul.

PETER: THE ROCK FOUNDATION OF THE CHURCH

In the Synoptic Gospels Simon (whom Jesus renamed Peter)
appears as a vigorous, enthusiastic, impulsive, somewhat naïve,
lovable, intensely human person. He is devoted to his Master,
yet his faith falters when he attempts to walk on the water, and
his loyalty is weaker than his concern for his own safety when
Jesus is on trial before the Sanhedrin. He is the first of the Twelve
to perceive that Jesus is the Christ, but, like the other Disciples,
he is decidedly slow—almost obtuse—in grasping the spiritual
meaning of the coming of the Messiah. Nevertheless, it is Peter
whom Jesus chooses to be the rock on which the Church will be
built.

---

* The rather inconclusive ending, leaving unfinished the story of Paul in
Rome, has led some commentators to believe that Luke intended to write
a third volume, which presumably would have told of the executions of Paul
and Peter and the persecutions of the Christians from A.D. 64 to 85 or 90.
For other explanations of the ending of the book, see Macgregor, *IB*, IX,
351-352.

In the book of Acts, Peter shows some of his former characteristics, but he is a changed man. He has been sobered by the Crucifixion and supremely reassured by the Resurrection. He has finally comprehended the meaning of the Incarnation, and he is able to explain it to an audience with great clarity and eloquence. His faith, his loyalty, and his courage are now invincible, so that he is willing to preach the Gospel even when doing so subjects him to imprisonment and flogging (and—if we may credit extra-Biblical tradition—ignominious martyrdom).

According to Acts, directly after Jesus' commissioning of the Apostles and his Ascension (1:1-14), Peter assumes the leadership of the 120 Christians in Jerusalem, thereby beginning the fulfillment of Jesus' promise to make him the foundation of the Church (Matt. 16:18).

Early Leadership (1:15-26). Peter's first act as leader is to address the little group of Christians, reminding them of the death of Judas Iscariot and proposing the election of a replacement among the "Twelve." * The group nominates two men, Barsabas and Matthias, and, after praying, casts lots and chooses Matthias as Judas' successor.

Sermon at Pentecost (2:1-41). When the Disciples meet in Jerusalem at the time of Pentecost,† there is a miraculous visitation of the Holy Spirit: there comes from heaven a sound "as of a rushing mighty wind," and "cloven tongues like as of fire" rest upon each man present. The Disciples begin to speak in "other tongues." A multitude of Jews of "every nation under heaven" gather to observe, and each man is amazed to hear the Disciples speaking in his own language.‡ When some skeptical spectators

---

* His version of Judas' death differs from that given in Matthew's Gospel (27:3-10). He says that after Judas bought a piece of land with his ill-gotten reward for betraying Jesus, he fell "headlong," and "burst asunder in the midst, and all his bowels gushed out."

† *Pentecost* (from Greek *pentekostos*, "fiftieth") is the Hellenistic term for the Jewish Festival of Weeks, celebrated fifty days after the Passover in thanksgiving for the "firstfruits" of spring harvest (see Lev. 23:15-21). Some groups of Christians observe this occasion (designating the day Whitsunday or Whitsuntide) in commemoration of the Apostles' Pentecostal experience as "firstfruits" of the working of the Holy Spirit after Christ's Ascension (*DB*, p. 1032).

‡ This is Luke's interpretation of the phenomenon known as "talking in tongues"—the unintelligible utterances of persons in a high state of religious

accuse the Disciples of being drunk, Peter arises to deny the charge and to assert that the Disciples are filled not with wine but with the Holy Spirit. His sermon which follows is an eloquent defense of Christianity.[8] He says that the Pentecostal phenomena are fulfillments of a prophecy (Joel 2:28-32) and that Jesus' life as the Messiah and his Resurrection and Ascension (of which many present can bear witness) are fulfillments of David's predictions (Psalms 16:8-11, 110:1, and 132:11). He urges all the Israelites to accept Jesus as the Messiah.

The First Christian Church: A Communal Institution (2:41-47). So persuasive is Peter's preaching that three thousand people are converted thereby to Christianity. All who believe in Christ now form a commune: they sell all their property and distribute the proceeds among the group as each member has' need. (See also 4:32-35.) They continue orthodox worship in the Temple and synagogues, but they also meet at the homes of the various members of the Christian community to pray and to "break bread" together (that is, to dine together; the breaking of bread is not yet a sacramental practice).[9] The Apostles teach them the Christian doctrine and perform many miracles. Day by day more converts join the Christian community.

Peter's First Conflicts with the Jewish Authorities (Chs. 3 and 4 and 5:12-42). Once when Peter and John * are entering the Temple, a man who has been lame from birth asks them for alms. Peter's response is famous: "Silver and gold have I none; but such as I have give I thee: In the name of Jesus Christ of Nazareth rise up and walk" (3:6). The man is immediately healed, and he enters the Temple, "walking, and leaping, and praising God." Many people see the former cripple and marvel at the miraculous cure. This is Peter's cue to preach a sermon, in which he tells them that the miracle has been performed through the power of Jesus, the resurrected Messiah, whom the Jews rejected

---

excitement. The phenomenon was common in Apostolic days (notice, for example, the references in Acts 10:46 and 19:6 and in I Cor. 12:10 and 13:1) and is still observable at the meetings of some of the more evangelical sects of Christians. See Macgregor, *IB*, IX, 37.

* Luke does not indicate which John is with Peter. Although it is generally assumed that John the Disciple is meant, Professor Kirsopp Lake has suggested that Peter's companion here is John Mark (Macgregor, *IB*, IX, 53-54).

and caused to be crucified. Again Peter exhorts the people to repent and believe. About five thousand are converted.

Hearing of Peter's deeds and teachings, the Sadducees arrest Peter and put him into jail for one night. The following day Annas (the high priest) and his relatives and other authorities question Peter and John, and again Peter delivers a sermon on Jesus and his Resurrection. The authorities warn Peter and John not to speak or teach "in the name of Jesus" and threaten them with punishment if they continue. The two Apostles, however, reply that they are taking their orders not from the Jewish leaders but from God himself. Annas and his cohorts, fearing the reaction of the people, refrain from punishing the Disciples and release them. The Christian community sings a hymn of praise and thanksgiving upon hearing of the two Disciples' victory (4:24-30).

More miracles and more conversions again provoke Annas to action.* He throws all the Apostles into prison, but the angel of the Lord releases them. Brought before the Sanhedrin, Peter delivers still another Christian sermon. The wise and tolerant Pharisee Gamaliel † advises against punishing the Apostles. He reminds the Sanhedrin of two former popular movements, led respectively by one Theudas and Judas the Galilean; both these men, Gamaliel says, died and their followers were dispersed.‡ If this new movement started by Jesus is "the work of men," it will pass away; but if it is God's work, then it cannot be overthrown, and the Jewish authorities would do well not to oppose it, lest they be, in effect, fighting against God. The councilors partially follow the advice of Gamaliel: after beating the Apostles, they free them. The Apostles rejoice in their opportunity to suffer for Christ, and they continue to preach and teach Christianity both privately and publicly.

The Judgment upon Ananias and Sapphira (5:1-11). Although most members of the Christian community in Jerusalem are, no

---

* This second clash (5:17-42) may be a doublet of the clash reported in 4:1-22. See Macgregor, *IB*, IX, 81.

† St. Paul's teacher. See Acts 22:3.

‡ It was the followers of Judas the Galilean who formed the nucleus of the group known as the Zealots; they subsequently were responsible for the insurrection which led to the destruction of Jerusalem in A.D. 70. (Macgregor, *IB*, IX, 87.)

doubt, "dedicated" and upright people, there are some back-sliders. Two such are Ananias (whose name has become a synonym for *liar*) and his wife Sapphira. Like other members, these two promise to give all their property to the community. When they sell a plot of land, however, they decide to keep part of the proceeds for themselves. Peter confronts Ananias with the accusation: "Ananias, why hath Satan filled thine heart to lie to the Holy Ghost, and to keep back part of the price of the land? . . . Thou hast not lied unto men, but unto God." Upon hearing Peter's words, Ananias falls dead. Three hours later Sapphira, unaware of her husband's fate, lies similarly about the price of the land; and she, too, falls dead.*

The Institution of Stewardship (Deaconship) (6:1-7). One very brief passage in Acts is nevertheless significant, for it is the Biblical authority for the modern appointment of deacons to administer the material affairs of certain Christian sects. When members of the Jerusalem group complain that some widows are being overlooked in the daily distribution of food,[10] the Apostles convene and decide that their own primary function of preaching the Gospel leaves too little time for them to attend to the physical needs of their followers. Therefore they appoint seven good and wise men to perform such services and formally ordain them by the "laying on of hands"—a rite symbolizing the bestowal of the Holy Spirit.†

Peter's Rebuke to Simon Magus (8:9-24). After Philip the Evangelist has converted many Samaritans to Christianity (see below, p. 79), Peter and John ‡ come to Samaria to perform the rite of laying their hands upon the new converts so that they will receive the Holy Spirit. One of these fledglings is Simon Magus (Simon the Magician), who not only enjoys great fame as a sorcerer but also probably has messianic ambitions.[11] When Peter approaches him, Simon offers the Apostle money in return

---

* This punitive miracle should be compared with the punishment of Achan (Joshua 7).

† This rite, derived from Old Testament practices (see, for example, Num. 27:23) is still practiced in the ordination of deacons, in Christian baptism, and in other rituals. See Macgregor, *IB*, IX, 90.

‡ Again Luke fails to say which John is meant. See Macgregor, *IB*, IX, 111.

for the power of "laying on of hands," thereby committing the sin which has adopted his name and is now known as "simony." *
Peter replies with a scathing rebuke: "Thy money perish with thee, because thou hast thought that the gift of God may be purchased with money." Simon repents and begs Peter to pray God not to inflict punishment upon him.

Peter's Cure of Æneas and Raising of Dorcas (9:32-43). Peter helps to spread the Gospel by performing miracles in two cities in western Palestine. In Lydda he cures the paralytic Æneas, and in Joppa he raises from the dead a woman named Tabitha (Greek, Dorcas).† The latter was formerly "full of good works and almsdeeds" and made many "coats and garments"—presumably to give to the poor; hence her name has been appropriated by "countless sewing circles" in modern times.[12]

Peter's Conversion of Cornelius the Centurion (10:1–11:18). While Peter is in Joppa, God sends a vision to Cornelius, a centurion of Caesarea ‡—a charitable and devout man. An angel appears to Cornelius, tells him that his alms and his prayers are to be rewarded, and directs him to summon Peter from Joppa. On the following day Peter, too, has a vision. While praying on a housetop, he falls into a trance and sees the heavens opened and something like a great sheet being lowered. In it are all kinds of "wild beasts, and creeping things, and fowls of the air." A voice instructs Peter to "kill and eat," but he refuses, because some of the creatures in the sheet are "common or unclean" according to Jewish law. The voice speaks again to him: "What God hath cleansed, that call not thou common." Three times this same thing happens, and then Peter comes out of his trance. While he is still pondering the meaning of his vision, the Holy Spirit tells him that three men are seeking him below and that he must accompany them. Upon descending, he discovers the messengers sent by Cornelius.

* Simony has come to mean "traffic in that which is sacred; specifically, the crime of buying or selling ecclesiastical preferment" (*Webster's New International Dictionary*).

† These miracles recall Jesus' healing of the paralytic and raising of Jairus' daughter (Luke 5:18-26 and 8:41-42, 49–56) and also some of the deeds of Elijah and Elisha (I Kings 17:17-24 and II Kings 4:32-37) (pointed out by Macgregor, *IB*, IX, 129).

‡ Caesarea was north of Joppa and on the Mediterranean coast. It was the capital of the Roman province of Syria.

Peter and "certain brethren from Joppa" accompany the three messengers to Caesarea, where the centurion has gathered a large group of kinsmen and friends. When Peter approaches, Cornelius falls at his feet, but Peter raises him and tells him: "I myself also am a man." Cornelius relates his vision. Then Peter is able to interpret his own vision of the unclean beasts: God was telling him that Gentiles as well as Jews are to be recipients of the Gospel—that no man is common or unclean if God has chosen to send salvation to him. Thereupon Peter gives Cornelius and his friends a brief history of Jesus' life and a summary of his teachings. While the Apostle is still speaking, the Holy Spirit descends on all who are listening, they begin to speak in tongues. and Peter commands that all be baptized.

This is an especially significant event in the history of the spread of Christianity, because when Peter returns to Jerusalem, he tells the Jewish Christians of his experiences and persuades them that God intends Christianity not only for the Jews but also for the Gentiles (11:18).

Persecution of Peter under Herod Agrippa I (Ch. 12). In order to please the Jews, King Herod Agrippa I * begins a persecution of some of the Christians under his rule. His first notable victim is the Apostle James, the brother of John. There is a very ancient tradition which holds that Herod also killed John.

Herod Agrippa has Peter arrested, imprisoned, and bound with chains. While Peter is sleeping in his cell between two soldiers, an angel awakens him and tells him to arise. The chains fall off, and Peter and the angel walk out of the cell; the iron gate leading into the city opens of its own accord, and Peter is free. He proceeds to the home of Mary, the mother of John Mark, a favorite meeting place of the Jerusalem group; indeed, many Christians are gathered together praying when Peter knocks at the gate. A young girl answers his knock and is so astonished to see him that she leaves him standing outside while she carries the glad news to those within the house. Peter continues his knocking

---

* It should be recalled that Herod Agrippa I, grandson of Herod the Great, was king over most of Palestine (under the Roman emperors Caligula and Claudius) during the period A.D. 41-44. Partially Jewish himself (see p. 4), he was in most respects a beneficent ruler. His persecutions of the Christians were probably a result of his zeal for Judaism. See Macgregor, *IB*, IX, 156.

and is at length admitted. He tells the group about his wonderful rescue, instructs them to relay the tidings to the other Christians (especially to James, the brother of Jesus, who has become leader of the Jerusalem group), and then departs "into another place," apparently to escape further persecution. Being apprised of Peter's escape, Herod has the prison guards put to death.

Herod himself is destined to die soon after this event. One day he dons his royal robes * and delivers an oration to the people of Tyre and Sidon. They raise shouts of flattery: "It is the voice of a god, and not of a man" (12:22). Because he accepts this praise (and evidently the deification of himself), God's angel smites him: immediately he is "eaten of worms" and dies. After his death the Christian Church prospers.

Except for a conference with the Apostles and elders in Jerusalem (15:6-29), this is Peter's last significant appearance in the book of Acts. According to tradition, he visited Corinth and Antioch in Syria and founded the church at Rome, where, during the Neronian persecutions (A.D. 64), he was crucified (head down, at his own request, for he felt himself unworthy of the sort of execution suffered by Jesus).[13]

STEPHEN: THE FIRST CHRISTIAN MARTYR (6:8–8:2)

One of the seven deacons of the Church in Jerusalem is Stephen, "a man full of faith and of the Holy Ghost." He is far more than a mere steward, for he performs "great wonders and miracles" and preaches with irresistible wisdom and spirit (6:8-10). So persuasive is he that he provokes the hostility of some Judaists who bribe false witnesses to accuse him of blasphemy. Brought before the Sanhedrin, Stephen, following Jesus' precedent, says nothing in his own defense; rather he delivers a long and somewhat irrelevant history of God's dealings with the Hebrews (7:2-50), ending (strangely and abruptly) with an account of Solomon's building of the Temple. After finishing the history, he makes a blistering denunciation of the Hebrews for having persecuted the prophets and for having caused the murder of Jesus.

Luke now presents a superb contrast of the furious conserva-

---

* According to Josephus, these robes were made entirely of silver. This historian gives a slightly different account of Herod's death. (DB, p. 1035, and Macgregor, IB, IX, 162.)

tives, who were "cut to the heart" and "gnashed on him with their teeth," and Stephen, calm, radiantly confident, looking "stedfastly into heaven" and seeing "the glory of God, and Jesus standing on the right hand of God." When he tells his accusers of his vision, they cry with a loud voice, stop up their ears, seize him, and cast him out of the city. There the mob (among whom is the earnest young Pharisee Paul) stones him.[14] Again like Jesus, just before he dies he asks that his executioners be forgiven: "Lord, lay not this sin to their charge."

PHILIP THE EVANGELIST (8:5-8, 26-40)

The "blood of the martyrs is the seed of the church."[15] The stoning of Stephen is the beginning of a "great persecution" against the Church in Jerusalem; consequently many Christian leaders flee from the city and find refuge "throughout the regions of Judaea and Samaria." Wherever they go, they preach the Word.

One of the first Christian missionaries to carry the Gospel into non-Jewish territory is a Greek-speaking Jew known as Philip the Evangelist.* He goes to the city of Samaria, where he preaches, performs miracles, casts out demons, and heals the sick and the lame. Multitudes gather to hear and to watch him, to rejoice over his wonderful cures, and to be baptized.

Some time later, directed by an angel, Philip journeys south to a point on the road from Jerusalem to Gaza. There he encounters "a eunuch of great authority under Candace, queen of the Ethiopians" (8:27). The eunuch is reading the well-known passage from Isaiah concerning the suffering servant (Is. 53:7-8). When Philip asks whether he understands the passage, the eunuch admits that he needs guidance. Philip seizes the opportunity to explain that Jesus Christ was that vicarious sufferer foreseen by the ancient prophet.† The eunuch believes Philip's teaching and is baptized forthwith. Philip is miraculously carried away to Azotus by the Holy Spirit.

---

* One of the seven deacons was named Philip (Acts 6:5). Whether Philip the Evangelist is to be identified with that deacon or with the Philip who was one of the original Twelve Disciples is uncertain. See Macgregor, *IB*, IX, 278.

† This is the first definite application of Isaiah's "suffering servant" prophecy to Jesus. See Macgregor, *IB*, IX, 115.

BARNABAS: MISSIONARY TO ANTIOCH
(4:36-37; 9:26-27; 11:19-30)

One of the most capable and lovable of the early Christian leaders—and one whose accomplishments probably deserve greater recognition than they generally receive today—is Barnabas, the kinsman of John Mark * and a missionary companion of Paul. A native of Cyprus, Barnabas has moved to Jerusalem and has been converted to Christianity. He is first mentioned in Acts 4:36-37, where he is shown selling all his goods and laying the proceeds at the feet of the Disciples. He next appears (9:27) as a sponsor of the newly converted Paul, who is regarded with suspicion by the Jerusalem Christians; Barnabas brings Paul before the Apostles and persuades them that the former persecutor of Christians is now a genuine believer and a bold preacher for Christ.

Following the martyrdom of Stephen, Christians from Jerusalem begin to carry the Gospel outside of Palestine—to Cyprus and Syria. One of the most important cities to which these missionaries go is Antioch in Syria, on the Orontes River. At one time the capital of the Roman province of Syria, it is the third greatest city of the whole Empire, surpassed in size only by Alexandria and Rome itself.[16] At first the missionaries preach only to the Jews of the city, but soon they carry their message to the Greek inhabitants, too. The Church at Antioch becomes so flourishing that the Jerusalem group considers it expedient to send Barnabas there as a sort of special ambassador. He is delighted with the state of the Church and exhorts its members to "cleave unto the Lord." He feels, however, that the task of leading so great a group is too much for himself alone. Remembering Paul's zeal and sincerity, he goes to Tarsus and brings Paul back with him. The two remain at Antioch for a year, preaching and teaching the people.†

---

* The King James Bible calls Mark "sister's son to Barnabas" (Col. 4:10), but the Revised Standard Version considers the relationship to be that of cousin. *DB* (p. 1032) says that Barnabas is the brother of Mary, the mother of Mark.

† So successful were the labors of Barnabas, Paul, and their successors that eventually the headquarters of the Christian Church were transferred from Jerusalem to Antioch; St. Peter, Ignatius, and Chrysostom are all

Somewhat later when the Christians in Jerusalem are suffering from a famine, the members of the Church at Antioch take up a collection and send it to Judea by Barnabas and Paul.

The remainder of the story of Barnabas is intertwined with that of Paul and will here be discussed as part of the Paul saga.

PAUL: APOSTLE TO THE GENTILES

Philosopher, theologian, orator, scholar, missionary *par excellence,* martyr for Christ—Paul is the most eminent figure in the New Testament except Jesus. More than half of Acts is devoted to an account of his deeds, and he himself is the author of nine or more Biblical epistles.

Although the book of Acts has little to say about Paul's early life, the following summary may be pieced together from autobiographical passages in his epistles and in his speeches (as recorded by Luke).

Paul (or Saul,* as he was first named) was born about A.D. 5 [17] in the Roman free city of Tarsus in Cilicia, the northwestern section of the Roman province of Syria. Although Jewish by birth, he inherited Roman citizenship, a fact which aided him in many crises. He was brought up to speak both *Koiné* and Aramaic.

When he was fifteen, he went to Jerusalem to study Judaistic law under the famous Pharisee Gamaliel (see above, p. 74). This period of training continued about six years. Returning to Tarsus, he may have spent several more years studying Greek philosophy and some of the Oriental mystery religions. It was perhaps during his residence in Tarsus that he learned the trade of tentmaking, or perhaps leatherworking (see Acts 18:3).

---

reputed to have served there as bishops. (Macgregor, *IB,* IX, 146-147.)

An interesting note (Acts 11:26) to the story about Barnabas and Paul tells that it was in Antioch that the term "Christian" was first applied to the followers of Jesus.

* His given name was Saul. "Paul" (from Latin *paulus,* meaning "little") may have been a nickname acquired as a child and suggested by his small stature; or he may have deliberately adopted it after the conversion of the Roman proconsul Sergius Paulus (Acts 13:6-12). He himself signs all his epistles "Paul." Luke takes note of the change of name in Acts 13:9 (see Hatch, *IB,* VII, 189). *DB* (pp. 1035-36) suggests that he changed his name because he believed that a Roman citizen named Paul would be a more acceptable missionary to the Gentiles than a Jew named Saul.

Although Luke makes no mention of it, Paul had some sort of physical affliction, which he refers to as "a thorn in the flesh" (II Cor. 12:7)—whence we have derived the now well-worn phrase. What the affliction was is not known.

Soon after the Christian community was organized in Jerusalem, Paul went again to Judea and became a leader in the persecution of the Christians. It is at this point that Acts picks up the thread of his life.

The following chronological chart (with probable or approximate dates) should be helpful in tracing the course of Paul's career: [18]

A.D. 5	Birth at Tarsus
20–26	Study in Jerusalem
26–32	Study in Tarsus
32	Conversion on the road to Damascus
32–35	Sojourn in Arabia
35–43	Preaching in Tarsus and elsewhere in Cilicia
43–44	Preaching with Barnabas in Antioch
44–45	Trip to Jerusalem during famine
45–47	First Missionary Journey
47–49	Residence at Antioch
49	Attendance at the Council of Jerusalem
49–51	Second Missionary Journey
51–56	Third Missionary Journey
56	Arrest in Jerusalem
56–58	Imprisonment in Caesarea
58–59	Voyage to Rome
59–61	Confinement in Rome
61–63	Journeys to Spain, Crete, Macedonia, and Greece
64–65	Execution in Rome

Participation in the Death of Stephen (7:58–8:1). The first reference to Paul in the book of Acts comes at the conclusion of the story about the stoning of Stephen: "And the witnesses [that is, the murderers] laid down their clothes at a young man's feet, whose name was Saul. . . . And Saul was consenting unto his death." This passage suggests that Saul was a ringleader of the frenzied mob that killed Stephen, and it gives a good view of him as a zealous defender of Judaism, intent on wiping out a movement which he considered to be heretical.

Conversion on the Road to Damascus (9:1-22). Still "breathing out threatenings and slaughter against the disciples of the Lord," Paul secures from the high priest letters authorizing the arrest and extradition of any man or woman in Damascus belonging to the "way" (a primitive term for Christianity [19]). Then comes the most important event in his life—an event that completely transforms him and redirects the course of his actions. En route to Damascus he suddenly sees a light shining from heaven, and he falls to the earth. A voice says to him: "Saul, Saul, why persecutest thou me?" He asks: "Who art thou, Lord?," and the voice answers, "I am Jesus whom thou persecutest: it is hard for thee to kick against the pricks." Astonished and trembling, Paul inquires what he must do. The voice tells him to go into the city, where his course will be told to him. His companions, speechless with amazement, hear the voice, but see nobody.* When Paul arises from the earth, he is blind. His companions lead him into Damascus, where he remains without food or drink for three days. Then a certain Christian named Ananias (not the famous prevaricator) is directed by God in a vision to find Paul and teach him the truth about Christ. Ananias obeys. Paul regains his sight, accepts the Christian message, and begins to preach the Gospel as ardently as he had formerly tried to suppress it.

Escape from Damascus (9:23-31). According to Luke's account in Acts, after the passage of "many days" the Jews of Damascus plot to kill Paul, but at night the Christians let him down over the wall of the city in a basket, and he escapes to Jerusalem.†

---

* There are two other accounts of Paul's conversion in Acts: 22:4-11 and 26:12-18. The details are very slightly different in the three versions. In 22:9 Paul's companions see the light but hear no voice. Four times Paul himself refers to his conversion: Gal. 1:15-16; I Cor. 9:1; I Cor. 15:8; and II Cor. 4:6.

† Paul gives a different version of this incident. In Gal. 1:17-18 he says: "Neither went I up to Jerusalem to them which were apostles before me; but I went into Arabia, and returned again unto Damascus. Then after three years I went up to Jerusalem to see Peter, and abode with him fifteen days." And in II Cor. 11:32-33 he tells the story of escaping from Damascus in a basket, but here he says it was King Aretas [of Nabatea]—not "the Jews"— who sought to kill him. Were the "three years" spent in Arabia (that is, the desert land southeast of Damascus) or in Damascus itself? Macarthur (p. 423) says that the time was passed in Arabia, where Paul could reconstruct his life and thinking.

This is the occasion (mentioned above) when Barnabas convinces the Apostles that Paul's conversion is genuine (9:27). After serving with the Apostles for some time in Jerusalem, Paul returns to his native Tarsus (9:30).*

First Missionary Journey—to Cyprus and Asia Minor (Chs. 13,14). Paul and Barnabas are now two of the five leaders of the Church at Antioch in Syria. These five are informed by the Holy Spirit, apparently through the medium of a prophet,[20] that Paul and Barnabas have been selected for a special mission. After the ceremony of the "laying on of hands," the two chosen ones set out on what is now recognized as the earliest missionary enterprise officially sponsored by a church group.[21]

Their first objective is Cyprus, the island where Barnabas was born. They land at Salamis, where they are joined by John Mark. The three preach the messiahship of Jesus in the Jewish synagogues of the city.

Proceeding to Paphos, the capital (and, incidentally, the site of a famous temple to the goddess Aphrodite, the "Cyprian queen"), they make a favorable impression on the ruler of the island, the proconsul Sergius Paulus. Their attempts to convert him, however, are opposed by a Jewish sorcerer named Bar-jesus (or Elymas). Paul calls down the punishment of the Lord on this "child of the devil," and the sorcerer is temporarily struck blind. Astonished at the miracle, Sergius believes Paul's doctrines (possibly it is to be assumed that he is baptized).

Considering their mission in Cyprus accomplished, the three friends leave the island and go to the mainland of Asia Minor. At Perga John Mark leaves them and returns to Jerusalem (13:13) —thereby beginning a rift in the friendship between his uncle Barnabas and Paul, a rift which is later to widen (15:36-41).[22]

The itinerary of Paul and Barnabas in Asia Minor is as follows: Perga, Antioch of Pisidia,[23] Iconium, Lystra, and Derbe. At the first two of these cities they convert many people, but they are driven from each place by the hostility of the non-Christian Jews. At Antioch of Pisidia, Paul delivers a typical synagogue sermon

---

* Luke does not say how long Paul remained there, but references in Paul's letters lead us to believe that for about eight years he preached the Gospel in Cilicia. Then Barnabas brought him to Antioch (see above, p. 80).

(13:16-42), which begins with the Israelites' exodus from Egypt and mentions Samuel, Saul, and David. Up to this point the audience listens in attentive agreement. Then, however, Paul turns to discussions of John the Baptist, Jesus, the Resurrection, and the forgiveness of sins; and he ends with a somewhat skeptical remark about the Law of Moses. The Jews leave the synagogue, but the Gentiles stay to hear more. On the following Sabbath when the Jews rudely interrupt Paul's preaching, he abandons hope of converting them: "Lo, we turn to the Gentiles" (13:46). It is significant that the Gentiles had come to the synagogue in search of the religious and moral teachings provided by Judaism.

At Lystra (modern Zoldera) Paul's healing of a lame man so amazes the inhabitants that they begin to worship the missionaries as gods; they hail Barnabas as Jupiter and Paul as Mercury —"because he was the chief speaker," and the priest of Jupiter even brings garlands and sacrificial oxen. Paul and Barnabas are so horrified at these actions that they tear their clothes and loudly deny their divinity.

Soon afterward some Jews from Antioch of Pisidia and Iconium come to Lystra to denounce Paul and Barnabas. The fickle populace now stone Paul, whom they formerly have tried to deify, and they leave him for dead. Paul revives, however, and he and Barnabas retrace their steps through Asia Minor, visiting the Christian groups which they have organized earlier. Then they return to Antioch in Syria.

The Council at Jerusalem (15:1-35). In the meantime, two serious questions have been threatening to cause a split in the ranks of the Christian Church: (1) Is it necessary for Gentile converts to be circumcised (in accordance with Jewish law) before they can be accepted into the Church, and (2) must the Gentile Christians observe the other Mosaic laws (such as those pertaining to "unclean" foods) in their social intercourse with Jewish Christians?

Matters are brought to a head when some representatives of the conservative, Pharisaic wing of the Christian Church in Jerusalem arrive in Syrian Antioch and teach that no one can be saved without first being circumcised. Paul and Barnabas stoutly deny this assertion and are delegated by the Church in Antioch

to go to Jerusalem and to lay their dispute before the Apostles
and the elders.

At a formal conference in the Holy City the "circumcision
party" again states its case. Peter argues eloquently and cogently
on the other side (15:7-11), maintaining that God intends the
Gospel for both Jews and Gentiles (as proved by His sending
Peter to Cornelius) and that faith in the Lord Jesus Christ is
the only requisite of salvation. Paul, Barnabas, and Jesus' brother
James (who apparently is president of the council as well as
the leader of the Jerusalem community) all speak in support of
Peter's argument. Next James suggests a compromise on the
second matter of contention: he moves that the Gentiles be urged
to abstain from sexual immorality and from eating "unclean"
food—this last, perhaps, out of deference to their Jewish fellow
Christians,[24] who might be offended by such practices.

The council endorses James' suggestions and incorporates
them in letters to the churches in Syria and Cilicia, and it dis-
patches Silas (later to become Paul's colleague on a missionary
journey) and another disciple along with Paul and Barnabas to
deliver one of the letters to the Church in Antioch.[25]

**Second Missionary Journey—to Macedonia and Greece (15:
36—18:28).** Paul's suggestion to Barnabas that they revisit the
churches they have established in Syria and Cilicia leads to a
"sharp contention" between the two old friends: Barnabas wants
to take John Mark with them, but Paul objects on the ground
that Mark deserted them during their previous journey.[26] Here
Paul and Barnabas part company for good. Barnabas and Mark
sail to Cyprus, and the former is not mentioned again in Acts.

Paul and Silas now set out on the Second Missionary Journey.
They pay visits of encouragement to Christian groups in various
cities (many of them not specified) in Syria, Cilicia, and Asia
Minor. The only notable event on this part of the tour is the
adding of Timothy (Timotheus) to Paul's entourage. Timothy is
a half-Greek, half-Hebrew Christian of Lystra (or perhaps
Derbe),[27] who becomes Paul's traveling companion. Paul, Silas,
and Timothy travel through Phrygia and Galatia, establishing
churches which increase "daily" (16:5).

Paul yearns to go first into "Asia"[28] and next into Bithynia,
but in both instances he is forbidden by the Holy Spirit to preach
in those regions. At Troas, a city near the site of ancient Troy,

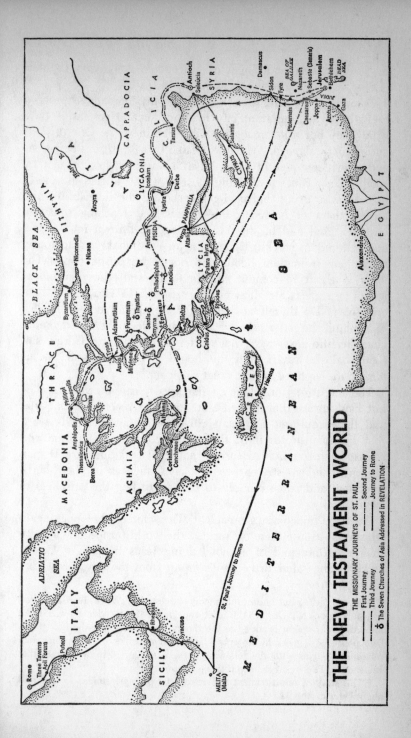

THE NEW TESTAMENT WORLD

THE MISSIONARY JOURNEYS OF ST. PAUL

— · — · First Journey ————— Second Journey
— — — Third Journey ————— Journey to Rome
⚲ The Seven Churches of Asia Addressed in REVELATION

he sees a vision of a "man of Macedonia" * praying to him: "Come over into Macedonia, and help us" (16:9).

Complying with the request, Paul and his companions proceed to Philippi, an important city in Macedonia. Here, as is their wont, they begin to preach the Christian message. One of their audience is a slave girl who is possessed by a "spirit of divination" and who consequently earns much money for her owners by soothsaying. Paul's exorcizing of this spirit angers the girl's owners, who bring the missionaries before the magistrates and accuse them of being trouble-makers and teaching unlawful customs. Paul and his friends are flogged, thrown into prison, and fettered in stocks. That night an earthquake miraculously frees them from their bonds and opens the prison doors. The jailer is about to commit suicide to forestall the punishment which he expects for allowing the prisoners to escape; but Paul cries out: "Do thyself no harm: for we are all here" (16:28). Trembling, the jailer asks what he must do to be saved. Paul's characteristic answer is: "Believe on the Lord Jesus Christ, and thou shalt be saved, and thy house." The jailer and all his family are baptized amidst great rejoicing.†

The magistrates order the missionaries' release on the next day, but Paul, aware that he and Silas have not received a fair trial and that scourging a Roman citizen is unlawful, sends word that the magistrates must themselves come to the prison and release them publicly. Hearing that Paul and Silas are Roman citizens, the magistrates fear the consequences of their harsh treatment and come humbly to the jail to beg the prisoners to leave the city.

Next the missionaries preach in Thessalonica, but once again "the Jews" accuse them of "turning the world upside down" with their doctrines and of acknowledging Jesus instead of Caesar as king. The rulers drive Paul's group from the city. Jews from

---

* An interesting but unprovable theory suggested by W. M. Ramsay (cited by Macgregor, *IB*, IX, 215) is that the "man of Macedonia" was Luke himself. Some weight is added to the theory by the fact that the first of the "we passages" (generally accepted as including Luke in the pronominal reference) begins with the following verse (16:10). It seems certain that Luke joined Paul's party at about this juncture.

† This story of imprisonment and release is strikingly similar to that told about Peter in Acts 12.

Thessalonica also follow them to Berea and "stir up the people" against them, so that they leave that place, too, and go on to Athens.

In this great city, formerly the very center of Greek culture, Paul is profoundly troubled by the people's idolatry. He speaks in the Jewish synagogues and arouses the condescending interest of some of the Epicurean and Stoic philosophers, who bring him to the Areopagus.* Here Paul delivers one of his most celebrated orations. He calls attention to the Athenian altar to "the unknown god" and announces that he can identify that deity for them: it is the Creator of heaven and earth and men, a God who does not dwell in man-made shrines, who commands men to repent, who has promised resurrection of the dead, and who will call men to account on a day of judgment. Paul's eloquence falls principally on skeptical ears. A few listeners, it is true, believe his teachings, but there is no New Testament record of an Athenian church, and "Athens may be said to be Paul's one significant failure." [29]

In contrast is Paul's eminent success in Corinth, a great, cosmopolitan port city. Here he is warmly received, and he converts many people. When Judaistic opponents accuse him of preaching an unlawful religion, the Roman governor Gallio finds him innocent. Because of the Jews' opposition, Paul declares that he will preach no more in the Corinthian synagogues, but will henceforth be an apostle only to the Gentiles.

After residing in Corinth a year and a half in the home of Aquila and his wife Priscilla, who are tentmakers, he decides to return to Syria. This pair accompany him as far as Ephesus, another large, cosmopolitan city, renowned as the site of a great temple of Diana; here the couple remain to try to spread the Gospel.† Paul himself goes back to Antioch in Syria.

---

* Either the hill famous as the scene of learned discussions or the Council of the Areopagus, which supervised educational and religious affairs of the city (Macgregor, *IB*, IX, 233).

† One of Aquila and Priscilla's converts is Apollos, a native Alexandrian and a disciple of John the Baptist. After his acceptance of Christianity he preaches the Gospel in Corinth, where some members of the church consider him a rival to Paul (see I Cor. 1:12 and 3:4-6). Martin Luther and others have attributed to Apollos the writing of the so-called Epistle to the Hebrews (*DB*, p. 1038).

The brevity of Luke's account of Paul's sojourn in Corinth (only eighteen verses) is misleading. Paul not only stayed there a long time but also made two later visits to the city and wrote at least four letters to its church.[30] These facts give a better indication of the importance of the Corinthian mission than does Luke's meager summary.

Third Missionary Journey—to Ephesus and Corinth (19:1—21:15). After spending "some time" in Antioch, Paul begins his Third Missionary Journey. First he revisits the churches in Galatia and Phrygia, "strengthening all the disciples." Faithful to a promise formerly made to the Ephesians (18:21), he now returns to Ephesus and brings the gift of the Holy Spirit to many who formerly were disciples of John the Baptist but who knew little or nothing about Jesus. After Paul has rebaptized them in the name of Jesus and has laid his hands on them, they "speak with tongues" and prophesy.

Reminiscent of the ambitions of Simon Magus are the practices of some Ephesian exorcists, who begin to use the name of "Jesus whom Paul preacheth" to cast out spirits. In one amazing instance seven sons of a Jewish high priest try this method. The evil spirit which they are trying to exorcize answers: "Jesus I know, and Paul I know; but who are ye?" (19:15); then the man possessed by the spirit attacks the seven exorcists and drives them from the house, naked and wounded. When news of this incident spreads, numbers of magicians make a bonfire of their books, and many people accept Christianity.

Resistance comes, as usual, from those with vested interests. Demetrius, a silversmith, angry because Paul's preaching is turning many Ephesians from the worship of Diana * and thereby reducing the sale of silver shrines and statues of Diana. Demetrius and his fellow artisans start a riot by shouting "Great is Diana of the Ephesians!" A mob forms; they seize two of Paul's companions and drag them to the theater. Eventually the town clerk calms the partisans of Diana; he advises Demetrius and his friends to prefer formal charges against Paul if they have any just complaint. The crowd disperses, and the matter is at an end.

---

* Diana of the Ephesians was a fertility deity and not to be identified with the Diana of Greek and Roman mythology, the sister of Apollo (*DB*, p. 1038).

Apparently after a long sojourn in Ephesus, Paul feels an inner compulsion to return to Jerusalem and thereafter to go to Rome (19:21). He makes a farewell tour of the Christian communities in Greece and Macedonia, stopping for three months at Corinth [31] and preaching a sermon at Troas "on the first day of the week" (20:7)—perhaps the first observance of Sunday (instead of the Hebrew Sabbath) as "the Lord's Day." [32] At Miletus he summons the elders and delivers a moving valedictory speech to them in which (20:17-35) he quotes the famous words of Jesus (which do not appear in any of the Gospels): "It is more blessed to give than to receive" (20:35). [33]

Despite a premonition of disaster (20:22-25) and subsequent warnings by the prophet Agabus and other friends (21:4, 10-12), Paul persists in his determination to go to Jerusalem.*

Arrest and Trial in Jerusalem (21:15—23:11). James the brother of Jesus together with other members of the Christian community in Jerusalem welcomes Paul and his fellow travelers, but they, too, warn Paul that his life is in danger. They suggest that, in order to mollify the Judaists, Paul pay the expenses involved in the ceremonies accompanying the completion of four Nazarites' vows and that he himself participate in the ceremonies.† Paul acquiesces,‡ but the Jews accuse him, nevertheless, of teaching against the Law and of trying to profane the Temple by bringing a Gentile (one Trophimus, an Ephesian) into the section of the Temple reserved for Hebrews. Again a mob forms, beats Paul, and intends to kill him. Rescued by Roman soldiers led by the tribune Claudius Lysias, he asks permission to speak to the people. His request being granted, he makes an appeal to the mob, in which he reviews the whole course of his life—birth, training under Gamaliel, persecution of the Christians, conversion, and missionary journeys. The people listen quietly

---

* One motive for Paul's return to Jerusalem was to deliver money collected from the churches in Greece, Macedonia, and Asia Minor for the relief of indigent Christians in Jerusalem. See I Cor. 16:1-4 and Rom. 15:26-28.

† See Num. 6:1-6.

‡ To some modern readers Paul's acquiescence has seemed inconsistent or even hypocritical, inasmuch as he had been preaching abroad that observance of the Jewish Law and ritual was unnecessary and that one needed only to have faith in Christ and his message. See Macgregor, *IB*, IX, 283-284, for a discussion of Paul's difficult role as an apostle to both Jews and Gentiles.

until he mentions the missions to the Gentiles; then they put on a violent demonstration, casting off their clothes, throwing dust into the air, and crying out that Paul is unfit to live. Again the tribune saves him. He prepares to scourge Paul, but desists when Paul proclaims himself a Roman citizen.

The next day the officer brings Paul before the Sanhedrin, now presided over by the high priest Ananias. When Paul addresses the members of the council as "brethren" and says that he has "lived in all good conscience before God" (23:1), Ananias orders attendants to strike him on the mouth. Paul's temper flares: "God shall smite thee, thou whited wall: for sittest thou to judge me after the law, and commandest me to be smitten contrary to the law?" (23:3). Perceiving that the council is made up of both Pharisees and Sadducees, Paul shrewdly causes a dissension between the two groups by revealing that he himself is "a Pharisee, the son of a Pharisee" and that he believes in the resurrection of the dead. The dispute becomes so violent that the Roman officer has to rush him to prison to prevent his being pulled to pieces. That night the Lord appears to Paul and comforts him by revealing that the Apostle will soon bear witness for him in Rome.

Imprisonment in Caesarea and Hearings before Felix, Festus, and Agrippa II (23:12–26:32). A group of the most fanatical of the Jews (presumably Sadducees) take a solemn vow not to eat or drink till they have killed Paul. They devise a plot: they will have Paul brought back before the Sanhedrin for further trial, and they will ambush him and murder him before he reaches the council chamber. Luckily Paul's nephew hears of the conspiracy and reveals it to Lysias, the Roman tribune. Apprehensive for Paul's safety, Lysias secretly transfers him to Caesarea with an immense escort of 470 soldiers. There Paul is placed in the custody of Felix, the procurator of the province of Judea.

The high priest Ananias, however, is persistent and sends a deputation to Felix to accuse Paul of subversive activities. Felix listens to the accusations and to Paul's defense, but decides to defer judgment till he can hear Lysias' version of the affair. Felix's wife Drusilla, a Jewess, persuades her husband to listen to Paul's doctrines. Felix is frightened by the Apostle's discourses on "righteousness, temperance, and judgment to come" (24:25).

Nevertheless, hoping for a bribe from Paul and desiring to please the Jews, Felix leaves the Apostle in military custody for two years.*

At the end of that time Felix is succeeded as procurator by Porcius Festus. Upon the suggestion of the Judaists of Jerusalem, who have planned another ambush, Festus considers sending Paul back to Jerusalem for another trial and asks for Paul's consent. Aware of the numbers of hostile witnesses in Jerusalem who are eager to testify against him, and perhaps perceiving the means to realize his ambition of going to Rome, Paul appeals to the Emperor Caesar.

At this juncture King Herod Agrippa II (son of Herod Agrippa I) and his sister Bernice † come to welcome Festus as the new procurator. Inexperienced as he is in Palestinian affairs, Festus lays Paul's case before the partly-Jewish Agrippa. Once again Paul tells the story of his life, including a detailed account of his conversion (26:12-18—the third account in Acts); he also argues that Jesus is the Messiah promised by the Hebrew prophets, and he proclaims that Christ rose from the dead and became a "light unto the people [the Jews], and to the Gentiles" (26:23). Such ideas are nonsense to Festus, who pronounces Paul mad. Paul protests that he is perfectly sane and appeals to Agrippa to corroborate his story. Perhaps scoffingly, Agrippa replies: "Almost thou persuadest me to be a Christian." ‡ Neither ruler, however, regards Paul as guilty of any crime, and Agrippa remarks that Paul could have been set free if he had not appealed to Rome.

Voyage to Rome (27:1–28:15). Paul and several other prisoners with a Roman centurion in charge of them set sail from Caesarea on a ship bound for Italy. Paul is treated with great

---

* Both Josephus and Tacitus agree with Luke in characterizing Felix as a corrupt and venal official. See *DB*, pp. 1039-40, and Macgregor, *IB*, IX, 307.

† Bernice later became the mistress of the Emperor Titus. Racine's tragedy *Bérénice* is based on a sentence from Suetonius concerning Titus' reluctant decision to give up Bernice as his legal wife and empress since Roman laws forbade the emperor's marrying a foreigner.

‡ The correct translation and interpretation of Agrippa's famous words ("In a short time you think to make me a Christian") are uncertain. Most modern exegetes agree that Agrippa was not really admitting that he had nearly been converted by Paul's words. See Macgregor, *IB*, IX, 330.

kindness and at Sidon is allowed to see his friends there (27:3).*
Against adverse winds, the ship arrives at Fair Havens, a port
in southwestern Crete, early in the fall (A.D. 55?). Because winter
voyages are dangerous, Paul advises waiting until spring to continue the journey; but since Fair Havens is not "commodious"
as a winter harbor, they try to reach another Cretan port.

Luke's account of the ensuing voyage is an exciting sea story,
even by modern standards, and it is also interesting for the light
which it throws on ancient nautical methods. The ship is struck
by a tempestuous northeast wind: "And when the ship was
caught, and could not bear up into the wind, we let her drive"
(27:15). The sailors are forced to lower the sails in order to
avoid striking sandbars. Being "exceedingly tossed with a tempest," they lighten the vessel by throwing some of the cargo and
tackle overboard. Sun and stars disappear for "many days," and
"no small tempest" lies on the ship, so that all aboard abandon
hope of being saved. Paul cannot resist an "I-told-you-so" ("Sirs,
ye should have hearkened unto me, and not have loosed from
Crete," 27:21) but reassures the sufferers that they will all
survive, for so he has been informed by God's angel. His prediction comes true: on the fourteenth night of the tempest the sailors
are able to sound the bottom. As they near an unknown shore,
they cast anchor and wait for day to come. The sailors begin to
lower a small boat over the side of the ship, but Paul thwarts
their attempted escape by revealing their plan to the soldiers,
who foolishly cut the boat loose and let it drift away. In order
for the passengers to reach land now, the ship must be beached.
The crew tries to beach it, but the bow sticks fast in a shoal and
the stern is shattered by violent waves. Some swim to shore,
others cling to boards and broken pieces of the ship, and all
reach land safely.

They find themselves on the island of Melita (Malta). The
natives treat them with great kindness and build a fire, for it
is raining and the weather is cold. As Paul is placing some sticks
on the fire, a poisonous viper fastens itself to his hand. The
Maltese assume that he is a murderer and that the shipwreck

---

* That Luke is one of the friends who accompany Paul on the voyage is
indicated by the use of "we" by the author of the passage; many descriptive
details in the account of the voyage seem to be the observations of an eyewitness.

and snakebite are retributive justice; but because he suffers no harm from the viper, they change their minds and proclaim him a god. His prestige is further enhanced by his curing many islanders who are ill.

Three months later Paul's party sets sail once more and eventually lands safely at Puteoli (Pozzuoli, on the Bay of Naples).[34] Thence the group makes its way by land toward Rome. En route Paul is greatly encouraged by a deputation of Christian "brethren" from Rome who have heard of his approach and have come to welcome him.

Paul in Rome (28:16-31). After arriving in Rome, Paul is allowed to live in his own (rented) house, under the guard of a soldier. Not permitted to go to the synagogue, as has been his custom in most of the cities, he calls the Jewish leaders of Rome to his house. There he explains to them why he is a prisoner—that he has broken neither Jewish nor Roman law but has antagonized some of the Jews by preaching about the Messiah, "the hope of Israel" (28:20). The Roman Jews say that they have received no bad reports about him from Judea and that they are eager to hear his message concerning the new sect. "From morning till evening" Paul expounds his message about God's kingdom, arguing that Jesus is the fulfillment of Old Testament prophecy. Although some of his hearers are convinced, others are not. Paul recalls to them Isaiah's comment on the obtuseness of the Jews; and he announces that henceforth the salvation of God is for the Gentiles, because they will listen.

For two years he remains in Rome, receiving all who will come to his residence, "preaching the kingdom of God, and teaching those things which concern the Lord Jesus Christ, with all confidence, no man forbidding him."

Here Luke's history breaks off, without telling the outcome of Paul's trial—if, indeed, Paul was ever actually tried. It seems likely that Luke would have reported an acquittal. Less likely is the assumption that, if Paul was found guilty of sedition and was executed, perhaps Luke decided not to record the event. Also unlikely is the explanation that the matters pertaining to such a trial were too well known for comment in a letter to Theophilus. Perhaps the best suggestion is that Luke wrote a third volume, or scroll, which has not been preserved.[35] At any rate, his narrative ends with Paul still flourishing in Rome.

6

The Gospel According to John:
The Most Philosophical Gospel

Seventeen centuries ago Clement of Alexandria recognized the uniqueness of John's story of Jesus: [1] "After the other evangelists had written the facts of history, John wrote a spiritual Gospel." [2] Its emphasis on the spiritual nature of Jesus as the divine Son of God, the incarnation of God himself, makes the book the most mystical and the most philosophical of the four Gospels.

AUTHORSHIP, DATE AND PLACE, SOURCES

From the second until the nineteenth centuries there was virtually universal agreement that the author of this extraordinary book was the Disciple John, the son of Zebedee; * and even today most Roman Catholics and many conservative Protestants adhere to this view of authorship. Early in the nineteenth century, however, certain Biblical scholars began to doubt the Johannine authorship; the matter soon became—and still is—the subject of heated dispute. Arguments against the traditional view are as follows: (1) The approximate date of composition (*ca.* A.D. 100) formerly accepted by many scholars is too late for the Disciple to have been the author; at that time he would have been at least a hundred years old, and besides, there is some evidence for believing that John had been killed by the Jews much earlier. (2) There is no convincing evidence that the Apostle John lived in Ephesus, where the Gospel is thought to have been written; indeed, there is evidence to the contrary. (3) Many second-century Christians showed doubt about the authorship of the

* The oldest reference to the Apostle John as the author appears in the Muratorian Fragment (*ca.* A.D. 170).

book; for example, the Alogi (a Christian sect which rejected the Logos doctrine) attributed the Gospel to the Gnostic Cerinthus; and Hippolytus of Rome (*ca.* A.D. 190-235) found it necessary to defend John's authorship. (4) Both Mark and Luke imply that the Disciple John was a Galilean, whereas there is impressive evidence that the author of the fourth Gospel lived in or near Jerusalem.[3]

Some modern theories are (1) that John provided the material for the book and one of his disciples did the actual composition; (2) that the author was John the Elder, of Ephesus, a prominent leader in the Asian Church; (3) that the book is anonymous; and (4) that it is a composite work by at least two hands.[4] Some critics believe that the author was a Jew; others contend that he was a Gentile.[5]

Study of the Dead Sea (Qumran) Scrolls (believed to have been written in the second century B.C.) has convinced some scholars that the the author of the fourth Gospel had some early contact with the Essenes.[6] Like them he believed that men must experience spiritual repentance before baptism. Many passages in Essene writings are strikingly similar to some in John's Gospel (including references to "children of light" and "walking in the dark," etc.). To some extent, however, the similarities in ideas and language may be attributed to the fact that the early Christians in southern Palestine communities shared with the Jews a common heritage from the Hebrews of Old Testament times. The significance of the Dead Sea Scrolls is the establishment of a direct link between the teachings of Jesus and the mainstream of Judaism. Prior to the discovery of the Scrolls, there had been a gap of a thousand years between the time of Jesus and the oldest text of the Masoretic Hebrew Bible (dating back only as far as the eighth century A.D.).

A strong case can be made out for the following theories about composition: (1) The Apostle John is to be identified with (a) "the beloved disciple" mentioned often in the Gospel and (b) the witness referred to in 21:24, who furnished the major portion of the material for the Gospel. (2) The real author was John the Elder (mentioned above), who was probably a disciple of the Apostle John and who also probably wrote the epistles I, II, and III John, but not Revelation (traditionally attributed to the Apostle John). (3) The book was edited by a person or a group of persons associated with the Church of Ephesus; the editor(s) added what is now Chapter 21, a defense of the authenticity of the contents of the book.[7]

Concerning the date of composition, until recently it was generally agreed that John's was the latest of the four Gospels. If the Disciple was the author, then a fairly early date—no later than A.D. 100—is indicated. The Gospel shows an apparent familiarity with Luke's writings and therefore probably should be dated after A.D. 95. It was well known in Christian and Gnostic circles by A.D. 130, a fact which suggests that by that date it had been in existence fifteen or twenty years. Evidence furnished by the Dead Sea Scrolls indicates that much of the doctrinal content of John may have been known to the Essenes well before the end of the first Christian century. Hence it is possible that the Gospel was written much earlier than has heretofore been supposed. It seems likely that the date of composition was fairly close to A.D. 95.[8]

Ephesus, Antioch in Syria, and Alexandria have been suggested as the place of composition. If the theory that the author was associated with the Essenes is correct, the Gospel *could* have been written in Palestine.[9]

The sources employed by the author (henceforth designated "John") were the Gospel of Mark, Zoroastrianism, and probably the Gospel of Luke and the lore of the Essenes. John was also acquainted with Platonic terminology and modes of thought and with the Greek doctrine of the Logos (discussed in the following paragraphs).[10]

PURPOSE OF THE FOURTH GOSPEL

The primary purpose of the fourth Gospel was to persuade its readers that Jesus of Nazareth was the incarnation of the Deity. John himself clearly asserts that purpose: "But these [words] are written, that ye might believe that Jesus is the Christ, the Son of God; and that believing ye might have life through his name" (20:31). In order to explain his convictions to people familiar with Greek philosophy and certain mystery cults, John resorted to the use of their own terminology. About 500 B.C. Heraclitus, of Ephesus, had employed the Greek word *Logos* (literally, "word" or "reason") to denote the ultimate rational principle regulating the universe. Early in the first century A.D. the Jewish philosopher Philo, of Alexandria, rejecting abstract and impersonal Reason alone as the ultimate principle, conceived of a personal and transcendent God, by whose will the world was created and is governed.[11] Philo applied the word *Logos* to a combination of (1) Heraclitus' "rational principle" and (2) the will of God as it makes itself manifest in the world.[12]

John perceived that by borrowing Philo's concept of the Logos he might make clear to the Greco-Roman world his own belief about Jesus' divinity. The Logos (the Word), he proclaimed, "was made flesh, and dwelt among us" (1:14); that is, Jesus was the incarnation of the Logos.

Such was John's primary aim. Three secondary purposes, in addition, may be discerned: (1) To combat orthodox Judaism and to saddle it with the blame for Jesus' Crucifixion. Sometimes John does not single out the Pharisees, the Sadducees, the elders, and the scribes as Jesus' enemies, but accuses "the Jews" in general of rejecting Jesus' message and of conspiring to bring about his death. (2) To refute the heresy that John the Baptist was the Christ. The Evangelist repeatedly subordinates the Baptist and has him acknowledge his own inferiority to Jesus: "I am not the Christ, but . . . am sent before him. . . . He must increase, but I must decrease" (3:28-30).[13] (3) To refute Christian Gnosticism (Docetism), which held that the body was evil and that Jesus was not a real incarnation of God's spirit, but that the Spirit entered Jesus' body at the time of his baptism and left it at the time of the Crucifixion. Futhermore, the Gnostics tried to reduce Christianity to a speculative philosophy and Christ to an abstract "divine principle." [14] John stresses the reality of Christ as a human being, who experiences normal human sorrows and physical ills (for example, his grief over Lazarus' death [11:33-36] and the "blood and water" that poured from Jesus' side, pierced after his death on the Cross [19:35]).

STYLE

John's style is that of a lofty and rather formal discourse. More concerned with theology than with biographical data, the Evangelist employs the "lecture-room technique." [15] Taking a hint, perhaps, from the writings of Plato, he often uses dialectic methods. John frequently tells of Jesus' asking a question of his Disciples or other followers, listening to their answers, and then

pointing out to them wherein they have been right or wrong—
always throwing some new light on the subject under discussion.
One of Jesus' favorite rhetorical devices (if we may rely on John's
account) was to seize upon a simple, everyday word in the conversation of an acquaintance and to change its meaning so as to
add some allegorical or metaphorical significance, thereby teaching some new truth. For instance, when he asks the woman at the
well in Samaria for some water to drink, he tells her: "Whosoever
drinketh of this water shall thirst again: But whosoever drinketh
of the water that I shall give him shall never thirst; but the water
that I shall I give him shall be in him a well of water springing
up into everlasting life" (4:13-14). Similarly, when the Disciples
bring him food, Jesus says to them: "I have meat to eat that ye
know not of . . . . My meat is to do the will of him that sent me,
and to finish his work" (4:32-34). Again, he deliberately gives
an ambiguous meaning to the word *temple*, using it to mean his
own body, when he says that he will rebuild the temple in three
days after it has been destroyed (2:19).

Christ's use of many "bold metaphors" [16] to describe himself
and his functions on earth is designated by commentators as the
"I am" style, characteristic of John's Gospel: "I am the bread of
life" (6:35), "I am the light of the world" (8:12), "I am the door
of the sheep" (10:7), "I am the good shepherd" (10:11), "I am
the resurrection and the life" (11:25), "I am the way, the truth,
and the life" (14:6), and "I am the true vine" (15:1).

Some of these metaphors illustrate another feature of John's
style—the frequency of key words: *believe* (4:21, 4:42, 5:47,
6:29, 10:38, 11:15, 11:48, 12:36, 14:1, 14:11, 16:30, 19:35, and
20:31); *life* (1:4, 3:16, 3:36, 5:24, 5:26, 5:29, 6:33, 6:48-53, 6:63,
10:10-11, 10:15-17, 13:37, 15:13, 17:30, and 20:31); *light*, 1:4,
1:6-9, 3:19-21, 5:35, 11:9-10, 12:35-36, and 12:46); *love* (3:16,
5:42, 8:42, 10:17, 11:5, 11:36, 12:43, 13:1, 14:15, 14:28, 15:9-10,
15:12-19, 16:27, and 17:23); and *truth* (1:4, 5:33, 8:32, 8:40, 8:44,
16:13, 17:19, and 18:37).

In order to obtain a clearer view of John's aims and techniques,
let us compare and contrast his Gospel with the three Synoptics;
let us examine what features and incidents all four Gospels have
in common, and let us see what John alters, what he omits, and
what he adds.

All the Gospels tell about John the Baptist's ministry, Jesus' healing of the son of the centurion, the controversies between Jesus and his enemies, the feeding of the five thousand, Jesus' walking on the water, the woman's anointing of Jesus, the cleansing of the Temple, the Triumphal Entry into Jerusalem, the trial and Crucifixion, and the Resurrection.

DIFFERENCES FROM THE OTHER GOSPELS

Now let us observe some respects in which John differs from the Synoptics. In the first place, the fourth Gospel is less narrative than the three earlier ones. As Clement's statement (quoted above) suggests, John is less interested in facts and events than in doctrine. It has been said that this Gospel is not so much a biography of Jesus as a commentary on the Christ's self-revelation —John's mystical and philosophical reflections on the *meaning* of the Incarnation.

Consequently John's "representation of the person and teaching of Jesus" [17] is very different from that in the other Gospels. In John there is less stress on the events of Jesus' life than in the Synoptics: here there are no accounts of his birth, infancy, youth, temptation in the wilderness, or agony in Gethsemane. In John, Jesus' teaching are less concerned with the Kingdom of God and with men's treatment of each other, and more concerned with the nature of Christ and his relationship to God. The Synoptics emphasize Christ's miracles of healing in order to demonstrate his compassion for men; John seems more interested in the miracles as "signs" of Jesus' divinity, and he almost invariably has Jesus draw a theological lesson from the performance of a miracle (for example, the feeding of the five thousand "is a sign of the spiritual food which Jesus gives to men," and the restoring of sight to a blind man "is a sign that He is the light of the world." [18] In John there is no dramatic realization by Peter that Jesus is the Christ; * instead Jesus reveals his divine nature at the beginning of his ministry; and there is no transfiguration in John because here "His whole life was a continual transfiguration." [19]

Specific differences between John and the other Gospels also include the following: (1) In the Synoptics the ministry of John

---

* But there is a parallel to Peter's confession as found in the Synoptics. Compare Mark 8:27-30 and John 6:68-69.

the Baptist ends before that of Jesus begins; in John they overlap.
(2) The Synoptics imply that Jesus' ministry takes place chiefly
in Galilee and Perea; John indicates that it is performed principally at Jerusalem at various times during Jewish festivals. (3)
In the Synoptics Jesus' ministry apparently covers a period of
about one year; in John, nearly three years. (4) In the Synoptics
the Last Supper is eaten on the Passover; in John, on the previous
night. (5) In the Synoptics Jesus cleanses the Temple only a few
days before his death; in John the cleansing is accomplished near
the beginning of his ministry.

When John differs from the other Gospels, it is usually impos-
sible to determine which account is historically more accurate.
In such cases it should not be assumed that John is wrong and
the other right merely because John is outvoted three to one;
it should be remembered that Matthew and Luke depended on
Mark, and John probably depended on equally valid sources.[20]

Other events found in one or more of the Synoptics but omitted
in John are: (1) the Virgin Birth (perhaps John feels that any
allusion to Christ's physical origin might weaken his thesis that
He is the Incarnate Word); (2) Christ's baptism (Christ has no
sins to be washed away); (3) the Temptation (this might be
interpreted as implying human weakness); (4) the institution of
the sacrament of the Lord's Supper (Jesus' teachings associated
with this sacrament in the Synoptics follow, in John, the miracle
of the feeding of the five thousand); (5) apocalyptic pronouncements (for John, Jesus has already come to judge the world and
he will send the Holy Spirit as Comforter in his stead when he
forsakes this earthly existence [see 16:7-11]); and (6) the Ascension (there is no need for Jesus to be transported to heaven,
because he always has been and always will be part of the
Godhead).

PROLOGUE: JESUS AS THE LOGOS (1:1-18)

The Gospel of John and the book of Genesis open with the
same words: "In the beginning . . ." The Evangelist chooses this
phrase because he knows that it will recall to his readers the
Scriptural account of Creation, and he wants to suggest that the
Christ is coeternal with God.[21] "In the beginning was the Word
[Logos], and the Word was with God, and the Word was God."
John the Baptist has been sent to testify that Jesus is the "true

Light, which lighteth every man that cometh into the world. . . .
And the Word was made flesh, and dwelt among us (and we
beheld his glory, the glory as of the only begotten of the Father,)
full of grace and truth" (1:9,14).

FOUR MIRACLES

John records only eight of Jesus' miracles, and four of these
do not appear (at least, in the same version) in any of the
Synoptic Gospels. He omits all exorcisms of demons and evil
spirits. Perhaps he felt it unnecessary to convince his readers of
Jesus' divine power by heaping sign upon sign; instead he seems
to have chosen a representative group (which would illustrate
various aspects of his thesis) and to have arranged them in
climactic order, beginning with a convivial social event, including the bringing of health to the sick and the bringing of light
into darkness, and ending with a negation of death.

Water Changed into Wine (2:1-11). According to John,
Christ's first miracle is not one of healing but is the providing of
wine for a joyous wedding celebration at Cana. When the host's
supply runs short, Jesus asks the servants to fill six large stone
jars with water. The steward pours from one of the jars and
discovers that its content is no longer water, but wine. He comments to the host that this wine is as good as the superior sort
usually served at the beginning of a celebration—not like the
inferior sort passed around near the end (when guests are too
drunk to notice the difference).[22]

The Paralytic in Bethesda (5:1-16). John's account of the
curing of a paralytic is perhaps a variant of Mark's similar story
(Mark 2:1-12). But there are notable differences in the two
versions. Only John tells (1) that at times an angel enters the
curative pool and troubles the waters; (2) that the man has been
paralyzed for thirty-eight years; and (3) that the healing takes
place on the Sabbath and thus antagonizes "the Jews." (However,
in Mark 3:1-5 Jesus does heal on the Sabbath a man with a
withered hand.)

The Man Born Blind (9:1-38). Another miracle which is sometimes said to be exclusive to John but which may be actually
another version of Mark's story of Blind Bartimaeus (Mark
10:46-52) concerns Jesus' restoring sight to a man who has been
blind from birth. According to John such a miracle is performed

at Jerusalem during the Feast of Tabernacles, and Jesus uses the incident as the occasion for delivering his discourse on himself as the Light of the World and on the blindness of the Pharisees.

The Raising of Lazarus (11:1-44). Perhaps the most dramatic and memorable of all Jesus' miracles is the raising of Lazarus from the dead. Mary * and Martha, Jesus' good friends who reside in Bethany (see Luke 10:38-42), send word to Jesus in Galilee that their brother Lazarus is dangerously ill. Although his Disciples remind him that the Judean Jews are hostile and so may seek to harm him, Jesus decides to go to Bethany. En route he tells the Disciples that Lazarus is already dead; this sad news is confirmed as soon as Jesus and his followers reach the home of the bereaved sisters. Martha laments that Jesus did not arrive earlier, for then he could have saved Lazarus' life. Jesus tells her: "Thy brother shall rise again." Misunderstanding his meaning, Martha says, "I know that he shall rise again in the resurrection at the last day." This statement of faith is Jesus' cue for delivering (as so often happens in John's Gospel) a self-revelatory pronouncement: "I am the resurrection and the life: he that believeth in me, though he were dead, yet shall he live: And whosoever liveth and believeth in me shall never die" (11:25-26). Martha worshipfully acknowledges her belief in him as the Christ, the Son of God, the Messiah. After much grieving and weeping, Mary, Martha, and Jesus proceed to the cave where Lazarus' body has been laid. Jesus asks that the stone in front of the cave be removed, but Martha objects: "Lord, by this time he stinketh: for he hath been dead four days." Nevertheless, Jesus has the stone moved away. After praying to God, he cries in a loud voice: "Lazarus, come forth." Immediately the dead man is restored to life, and the bystanders release him from his grave-clothes.[23]

The miracle causes many spectators to believe in Jesus, but it also alarms the Pharisees and chief priests, who fear Jesus' power and therefore begin to plot against his life.†

* As mentioned above, John (11:2) identifies Mary with the woman who anointed Jesus and bathed his feet with her tears (see Luke 7:37-38).

† This is one of the rare instances in which Jesus specifies certain groups of "the Jews" as Jesus' adversaries. John uses this miracle (instead of the cleansing of the Temple, which he places early in Christ's ministry) as the climax of Jesus' conflict with "the Jews"—the event which leads directly to the Crucifixion.

RELATIONS WITH NICODEMUS * (3:1-21; 7:45-53; 19:38-40)

Nicodemus, a Pharisee and a member of the Sanhedrin ("a ruler of the Jews"), pays a secret visit to Jesus in the night. He accepts Jesus' miracles ("signs") as proof that Jesus is a "teacher come from God." It is obvious that his purpose is to learn the solution of an overwhelming religious problem, but Jesus anticipates his question and gives him an answer before he can speak: "Verily, verily, I say unto thee, Except a man be born again, he cannot see the kingdom of God." This is one of those cryptical, provocative sayings of Christ found so often in John's Gospel. Nicodemus can make nothing of the oracle and asks, "How can a man be born when he is old? can he enter the second time into his mother's womb, and be born?" Jesus explains that to "be born again" means to undergo a spiritual transformation—specifically, to accept Christ as the incarnate Logos and to obey his teachings concerning the New Covenant. Just as the snakebitten Israelites of old were healed by looking upon Moses' brazen serpent (Num. 21:9), so may every man be cured of his sinfulness by viewing Christ on the Cross ("lifted up," John 3:14) and believing on him. "For God so loved the world that he gave his only begotten Son, that whosoever believeth in him should not perish, but have everlasting life" (3:16).† Jesus goes on to explain that a man acts in accordance with his beliefs and therefore acts righteously if he really believes in the Christ.

Nicodemus appears twice more in John's narrative.

Once during a meeting of the Pharisees and chief priests, some of the Pharisees chide the Temple police ("officers") for not arresting Jesus. Nicodemus bravely speaks up: "Doth our law judge any man, before it hear him, and know what he doeth?" (7:51). The other Pharisees accuse him of being a follower of

* John alone mentions a person by the name of Nicodemus, but possibly he is the rich young man (Mark 10:17, Matt. 19:16) or rich ruler (Luke 18:18) who asks Jesus how he can attain "eternal life." John's phrase "kingdom of God" (found only once in this Gospel—in 3:3) is equivalent to the Synoptists' "eternal life" (Howard, *IB*, VIII, 504-506). The lesson following the encounter with the rich young man differs from that in John.

† Martin Luther called this famous verse "the Gospel in miniature" (Howard, *IB*, VIII, 510). Alice Parmelee (in *A Guidebook to the Bible* [New York: Harper and Brothers, 1947], p. 209) calls the verse the very heart "of this Gospel, and indeed of the Bible itself."

Jesus and reassure him that no Galilean can ever be a "prophet."

After the Crucifixion (19:39) Nicodemus brings a large quantity of spices ("myrrh and aloes") with which to embalm Jesus' body.

The three passages dealing with Nicodemus reveal him to be an earnest and conscientious man, sincerely seeking the truth, but hampered by the narrow and reactionary groups of which he is a member. He evidently fears the opinions and the power of these groups, for he first seeks Jesus secretly; apparently he remains silent when the other Pharisees scoff at him for being one of Christ's followers, and there is no evidence that he defends Jesus during the trial before Caiaphas.

THE WOMAN AT THE WELL IN SAMARIA (4:1-29)

Once while traveling through Samaria, Jesus is resting beside a well in the town of Sychar and asks a Samaritan woman for a drink of the water she is drawing. The woman inquires why he, a Jew, would condescend to beg a favor of a Samaritan. Ignoring her jibe, Jesus makes another of his enigmatic pronouncements. He tells her that if she had known to whom she was speaking, she would have asked *him* for a drink, and he would have given her living water. Failing (like Nicodemus) to grasp his meaning, she asks how he could draw water, inasmuch as he has no bucket or rope. Jesus replies that the water of which he speaks quenches a man's thirst permanently and leads to eternal life; that is, his "water" is spiritual truth. When (apparently with supernatural knowledge) he remarks that she had five husbands and is now living with a sixth man, she is convinced that he is a prophet. She seeks information, therefore, about another religious matter: the Samaritans worship God "on his mountain" (Gerizim), but the Jews insist on Jerusalem as the proper center of their religion. Which group is right? Jesus answers that the time has already come when the place of worship has ceased to matter; as long as man recognizes God as a universal Spirit and worships him "in spirit and in truth," the locale is of no importance. The woman says that she believes in the coming of the Messiah, who will solve all these problems. Then Jesus says: "I that speak unto thee am he." Astounded by this revelation, the woman forgets her waterpot and hastens into the city to spread the good news.

THE WOMAN TAKEN IN ADULTERY ° (8:1-11)

The compassionate and forgiving side of Jesus' nature is shown
in John's account of an incident involving adultery. A woman has
been caught in the sinful act, and the scribes and Pharisees bring
her before Jesus for judgment—not because they really regard
him as an authority, but because they hope to trick him into
saying something that will antagonize the people or the Roman
overlords. If Jesus should tell them to kill her (in accordance
with the Mosaic law, Lev. 20:10 and Deut. 22:22), the Pharisees
could report him to the Roman rulers for inciting others to commit murder; but if Jesus decreed that the woman should go
free, he would be flouting the Hebrew law.[24] Again (as often
in Mark and Matthew) Jesus perceives the evil designs of his
enemies and easily escapes between the horns of the dilemma.
He stoops, writes in the sand with his finger,† and says: "He
that is without sin among you, let him first cast a stone at her."
Convicted by their own consciences, the accusers shamefacedly
depart one by one, and Jesus and the woman are left alone. He
asks whether any sentence has been passed upon her, and she
answers in the negative. Jesus tells her: "Neither do I condemn
[pass sentence on [25]] thee: go, and sin no more" (8:11). Jesus is
not condoning the woman's actions, of course, but is demonstrating God's mercy and forgiveness to repentant sinners who will
endeavor to mend their ways.

TWO ALLEGORIES

It has been mentioned that although John records none of the
parables, which are highly important in the Synoptics, he does
preserve much allegorical and metaphorical language used by
the Master. Two famous "allegories" (as most commentators label
them) are the following:

° This famous story is not found in the "best" manuscripts of John, and
in the Revised Standard Version it is relegated to the marginalia. It is more
characteristic of Jesus as he is portrayed in the Synoptics than as he is
usually portrayed by John.

† There has been much speculation about what it was that Jesus wrote in
the sand. W.A. Smart (in a lecture at Emory University) has suggested that
Jesus was embarrassed in behalf of the poor woman and merely scribbled
to hide his embarrassment.

The Good Shepherd (10:1-18). "I am the good shepherd," Jesus asserts (10:11). A good shepherd is one who enters the sheepfold by the door, calls his sheep by name, leads them to the pasture, and stands willing to lay down his life for them. Jesus emphasizes the point that he will lay down his life for his sheep—those who believe in him and obey his commandments. The enemies who will kill him are mere instruments of God the Father; the will of the Son and that of the Father are the same. The good shepherd is contrasted with a thief, who climbs surreptitiously into the fold to steal and to destroy. Jesus says that the many professed teachers who have preceded him (the false prophets, false Messiahs, and fanatical Zealots [26] are "thieves and robbers." The good shepherd is also very different from the hireling, who flees whenever danger threatens the sheep. In the middle of the allegory Jesus changes the figure and calls himself "the door," through which one must enter if he wishes to be saved (to "go in and out, and find pasture"—10:9).

The True Vine (15:1-11). In the allegory of the True Vine, Christ likens God the Father to a vinedresser ("husbandman"), himself to a vine, and all his followers to branches of the vine. As a vinedresser removes unfruitful branches and burns them, so will God remove men who fail to love and serve him; and as the vinedresser prunes good branches to make them more fruitful, so he will chasten and cleanse the righteous that they may become more righteous. As for the Disciples, they have already been cleansed; insofar as they "abide" in Christ and he in them, they will produce good works. This allegory has been called John's "most complete expression of the mystical union between Christ and the Christian." [27]

THE SCOPE OF CHRIST'S MISSION (12:20-36)

"Certain Greeks" (apparently proselytes to Judaism, for they have come to Jerusalem to celebrate the Passover) approach Philip and ask for an introduction to the Teacher, whose fame is now widespread: "Sir, we would see Jesus." The request is relayed to the Master (12:22), and then no further mention is made of the Greeks; John fails to say whether or not Jesus converses with them. The mere fact that news about the Messiah has reached the Gentiles seems to be for John a "prophecy of the universal spread of Christianity," [28] and for Jesus a signal that the fulfillment of his mission on earth is at hand: "The hour is come, that the Son of man should be glorified" (12:23). Just as a grain of wheat must fall into the ground and suffer dissolution in order to produce more grain, so Christ must die in order to live again and thereby carry out God's purpose. Such self-sacrifice, he says, is every man's way to salvation: "He that loveth his life shall lose it; and he that hateth his life in this world shall keep it unto life eternal" (12:25).*

Here John differs slightly from the other Gospels. Whereas in Mark 14:36 Jesus asks God to spare him the impending suffering of the Crucifixion, John quotes him as saying: "What shall I say? Father, save me from this hour: but for this cause came I unto this hour" (12:27). The culmination of the Incarnation is his Atonement on the Cross for the sins of the world, and his Resurrection is to be proof to all men that they; too, can inherit eternal life. Therefore Christ prays: "Father, glorify thy name" (that is, by carrying out the divine plan).† A voice from heaven answers: "I have both glorified it, and will glorify it again" (12:28).‡ Jesus announces that the Judgment Day is at hand, that Satan shall be cast out, that he himself will be taken away from the earth, and that he will draw all men unto himself. His hearers again fail to comprehend his meaning and quote the Law to the effect that the Christ will remain forever. Ignoring their objection, Jesus warns them that this is the crucial time: they must believe *now* in the light while it is with them, so that they may attain salvation.

SERMON OF LOVE AND COMFORT (13:1–16:33)

The doctrinal and emotional climax of John's Gospel comes in the form of a farewell sermon to the Disciples on the occasion of the Last Supper. After washing the Disciples' feet as an object lesson in humility and in service to others (13:1-17), Christ again predicts his imminent departure from them. He commands them to love one another in the same way that he has loved each

* Compare Jesus' advice to the Disciples in Mark 8:35, Matt. 10:39, and Luke 9:24.

† This is the equivalent to the prayer in Mark: "Nevertheless not what I will, but what thou wilt" (14:36).

‡ Compare the voice at Jesus' baptism (Mark 1:11) and the voice at the Transfiguration (Mark 9:7).

of them, so that people will recognize them as his followers after he has gone. Peter declares that he will follow wherever Christ goes, even if it should mean death. Jesus says that Peter may follow him later, but not now (perhaps in "prophetic" allusion to the martyrdom of Peter [29]), and he predicts the Apostle's three denials (as in Mark 14:30).

Perceiving the anxious expressions on the faces of the Disciples, Jesus speaks words of assurance to them—words which all future generations have considered the most comforting passage in the Bible (Ch. 14), beginning, "Let not your heart be troubled." He tells them that he will come again after death and take them with him so that they may always reside with him in heaven. He has shown them the way already: *he* is "the way, the truth, and the life" which alone can lead men to the Father, for he and the Father are one and the same. He promises to send the Holy Spirit to comfort all men while he (the Son) is absent and to make himself manifest to all men who keep his commandments.

After the allegory of the True Vine (15:1-11), he again enjoins the Disciples to love every human being, even as he has loved all men: "Greater love hath no man than this, that a man lay down his life for his friends" (15:13).

Warnings of persecutions and more promises of comfort follow. The discourse ends with the triumphant declaration: "These things I have spoken unto you, that in me ye might have peace. In the world ye shall have tribulation: but be of good cheer; I have overcome the world" (16:33).

7

The Epistles of Paul*

The great "missionary to the Gentiles" tells us that he was not considered especially eloquent as a preacher, but that his epistles were effective: "For his letters, say they, are weighty and powerful; but his bodily presence is weak and his speech contemptible" (II Cor. 10:10). One must bear in mind that these letters were written not for publication, but for the purpose of solving the problems of specific churches and a few particular individuals. Many of them were occasioned by communications from the churches which Paul had established in Asia Minor and in Greece. Paul probably knew, however, that the letters to the churches would be read in public, passed from church to church, and preserved as precious religious documents. Therefore, he planned the letters (at least some of them) studiously and chose his diction with the greatest care. His style varies from the calmly and coldly logical (as in the passages in Romans about the law and election) to the emotional and poetic (as in the hymn to immortality in I Cor. 15).

It is believed that Paul dictated most of his letters either to public stenographers or to friends and then added some personal words of greeting in his own hand.

Pauline authorship is now generally accepted for Romans, I and II Corinthians, Galatians, Ephesians, I and II Thessalonians, Philippians, Colossians, and Philemon, although some critics contend that Ephesians and II Thessalonians were written not by Paul but by his disciples. Although the so-called "Pastoral Epistles" (I and II Timothy and Titus) were probably based on notes by Paul, in their present form they must be dated well after the death of the great Apostle. As for Hebrews, no responsible

* For the life and ministry of Paul, see the discussion under the Book of Acts, pp. 68-95.

scholar now attributes it to Paul, and there is considerable doubt as to whether it should even be classified as an epistle.

Paul's epistles were written in the latter half of his career. The date of composition of each letter (discussed separately below) is conjectural; therefore, the order followed in this Outline must be considered tentative.

THE EPISTLES TO THE THESSALONIANS

The book of Acts (16:9—17:34) records how Paul and his assistants established Christian communities in the Macedonian cities of Philippi, Thessalonica (modern Salonica), and Berea and how the opposition of "the Jews" forced them to flee each of these cities in turn.* After journeying to Athens and then to Corinth, Paul wrote two letters to the young church at Thessalonica, the principal city of Macedonia, offering encouragement and advice.

The First Epistle to the Thessalonians: A Promise of Immortality. Paul's first letter to the Thessalonians probably bears the distinction of being the oldest Christian writing in existence. (Some scholars think that the letter to the Galatians precedes it.) It was written about A.D. 51.

Worried over the spiritual welfare of the new Christian communities in Macedonia, Paul was apparently planning to return when he was stricken by one of those seizures to which he was subject: "Satan hindered us" (I Thess. 2:18).† Hence he sent his colleague, Timothy, in his stead to encourage the community at Thessalonica and to bring him word of its welfare. Timothy's return to Corinth with good news is the occasion of this epistle.

Its merits are clarity, simplicity, and the revelation of the intrepidity, affection, intensity, and missionary zeal of its author.

SALUTATION AND PRAISE (Chs. 1–3). After a brief and conventional salutation from himself, Silas ("Silvanus"), and Timothy, Paul congratulates the church at Thessalonica for its fidelity. He reminds the congregation of the diligence and disinterestedness with which he and his companions labored for this new Christian community, and he urges the members to persevere in the faith.

MORAL INJUNCTIONS (4:1-9). While in Thessalonica, Paul had apparently confined his preaching to an exposition of the basic

---

* For a summary see pp. 88-89 above.

† Compare his reference to his "thorn in the flesh," II Cor. 12:7.

Christian beliefs about Jesus' Messiahship, death, and Resurrection (Acts 17:3). Perhaps he had had little opportunity to explain the moral implications of the Gospel, or perhaps the Thessalonians had not heeded them. At any rate, in Chapter 4 Paul exhorts the new converts to abstain from sexual immorality, to practice the Christian virtues of selflessness and brotherly love, to "work with their hands," and to live quietly and unobtrusively.

IMMORTALITY AND THE SECOND COMING (4:9—5:11). Next, Paul answers two questions which seem to have been bothering the Thessalonians: first, will Christians who died before Jesus' Second Coming achieve immortality; and, second, when will Jesus return to establish his Kingdom? In answer to the first, he assures them that *all* who believe in Jesus will inherit eternal life; indeed, the "dead in Christ shall rise first," and those who are still alive "shall be caught up together with them in the clouds, to meet the Lord in the air" (4:16-17). As for the time when these things will be, nobody knows, for "the day of the Lord so cometh as a thief in the night" (5:2); Jesus' true followers are not to worry about such matters but to remain ever in readiness for the glorious event.

CONCLUSION (5:11-28). After a few more moral precepts and a request that the letter be read "to all the brethren," the letter closes with a benediction.

The Second Epistle to the Thessalonians: A Warning against Idleness. Soon after he had written the First Epistle to the Thessalonians and apparently while he was still in Corinth with Silas and Timothy (probably about A.D. 51), Paul learned that the Christian group at Thessalonica was continuing to encounter bitter opposition from "the Jews." An equally serious threat arose from within: some members were taking Paul's prediction of Jesus' Second Coming so seriously that they considered it unnecessary to carry on their customary labors. Paul's second letter to the Thessalonians deals with these two problems.

Because of the similarity of the messages of I and II Thessalonians and because the content of the second is rather apocalyptic, some scholars have doubted its Pauline authorship. Others have suggested that, though Paul may have written it, it was originally addressed to some other young church, perhaps the one at Berea. However, the consensus today is that Paul wrote it to the Thessalonians.

SALUTATION AND PRAISE (Ch. 1). First, Paul congratulates the church on its fortitude in the face of afflictions and persecutions, and again he exhorts its members to stand fast in the faith.

WARNING AND EXHORTATION (2:1—3:16). Next, Paul warns them that though they should eagerly await the Second Coming, it is not yet at hand, and no one knows exactly when it will. It will be preceded by a great battle between the powers of evil, led by the Antichrist ("the man of sin," 2:3), and the forces of good.* Paul has little patience with those who use the imminence of the Second Coming as an excuse for shirking their duties— mere "busybodies": "For even when we were with you, this we commanded you, that if any would not work, neither should he eat" (3:10). He urges them again to work quietly, eat their own bread, and "be not weary in well doing" (3:13). Here Paul exhibits that "rare blend in his character of high spiritual ardor and practical wisdom." [1]

CONCLUSION (3:17). An interesting "polite close" is evidence for the letter's authenticity: "The salutation of Paul with mine own hand, which is the token in every epistle: so I write" (3:17).

THE EPISTLES TO THE CORINTHIANS

After a dismal missionary failure in Athens (see p. 89), Paul went to Corinth, apparently intending to stay only a short while and then return home. Although it was "in fear, and in much trembling" (I Cor. 2:3) that he entered that great cosmopolitan city, noted for its worldliness, paganism, and licentiousness, he found the response of the Corinthians to the Gospel so enthusiastic and so enduring that he remained with them nearly two years, and the church at Corinth became one of his favorites. His letters to its members consitute the largest block of correspondence addressed to any one church; and they are especially significant for (1) their autobiographical content, (2) their theological doctrines, and (3) their reflection of life in a first-century Christian community. Of the highest literary value, these epistles range in tone from the coolly practical to the almost ecstatic, and in subject matter from specific mundane problems and per-

---

* This belief was an important element in early Christian apocalyptic literature; compare Mark 13:14; Matt. 24:15; I John 2:18 and 4:3; and especially Rev. 12–20. For other apocalyptic passages by Paul, see I Thess. 4:16—5:3 and I Cor. 2:6, 7:29-31, and 15:51–57.

sonal grievances to such exalted themes as the Atonement and personal immortality.

Scholars have long been puzzled over the number of letters addressed by Paul to the Corinthians. Their length and their desultory nature (especially of I Corinthians) suggest that perhaps our version consists of many epistles, written over a period of at least a year. A personal letter, however, is likely to pass rather casually from one subject to another; and there is good reason to suppose that Paul would include his opinions about a number of topics in any one epistle. Many authorities, nevertheless, recognize four distinct letters or fragments, composed in the following order: (1) II Corinthians 6:14—7:1; (2) I Corinthians; (3) II Corinthians 10–13; and (4) II Corinthians 1:1—6:13 and 7:2—9:15. All appear to have been written from Ephesus, about A.D. 53-54.

The Second Epistle to the Corinthians: A Fragment concerning Paganism (6:14—7:1). In I Corinthians 5:9-11, Paul refers to an earlier letter in which he has warned against unnecessary associations with immoral men. It seems likely that a fragment of this earlier letter was accidentally inserted into the midst of what is now II Corinthians so as to cause a rather startling interruption of a charming passage on reconciliation. The fragment advises the readers not to be mismated with non-believers, for one may become unclean by touching the unclean.

The First Epistle to the Corinthians: Solutions and Reassurances. The Greek penchant for philosophical truth-seeking and tendency toward disunity and individuality gave rise to many problems when the Corinthians embraced Christianity.[2] They found difficulty in understanding Jesus' conception of God and of the afterlife and in applying Jesus' teachings to their own personal ethics. It seems that sometimes they wrote to Paul for solutions, and sometimes Paul heard about their bickerings and backslidings through other sources. In I Corinthians, with no attempt at logical arrangement, he deals with one problem after another.

Some of these topics are of minor interest today. But we should note that in offering solutions to problems which are no longer current or which seem trivial to us, Paul often gives advice of permanent significance. For example, when he deals with the problem of whether a Christian should eat food sacrificed to an idol, he warns that one should be careful to avoid all things which, though harmless to himself, might cause his neighbor to sin.

FACTIONS WITHIN THE CHURCH (Chs. 1-4). It has been reported to Paul that the members of the Corinthian church have split into factions, some claiming to be followers of Peter (Cephas), others of Apollos (an eloquent missionary), and others of Paul himself. Paul refuses to take part in these controversies, probably because he has discovered in Athens that disputation "on the level of logic and rhetoric" are futile; therefore "he moves the discussion to the plane of sheer religious experience." [3] He has come to them with "the things of the spirit" which "are spiritually discerned." This is "the wisdom of God," which is considered mere foolishness by the "wise in this world." Let the Corinthians stop bickering about schools of thought and loyalties to any human leaders, and let them remember only that God is not divided and that they are all laborers for Him.

EXCOMMUNICATION OF EVILDOERS (Chs. 5:1-13 and 6:9-20). In Chapter 5 (and also in II Cor. 6:14-17) Paul urges the excommunication of wicked members of the church—the sexually immoral, the greedy, robbers, idolators, revilers, and drunkards. This disciplinary weapon, to become especially powerful in the Roman Catholic Church during the Middle Ages, was not, in fact, a new measure, but one which was recognized by Jewish law (Deut. 21:21 and 22:21), and used by the Judaists against the Christians (John 9:22).

Paul especially warns against sexual immorality, for the body is a "member" of Christ and a temple of the Holy Spirit. Therefore each Christian should "glorify God" in his body.

LAWSUITS AMONG CHURCH MEMBERS (Ch. 6:1-8). In a brief but significant passage, Paul admonishes the Corinthians to settle their disputes among themselves without resorting to a court of law. It would be better in his view for a church member to suffer injustice than to air his grievances before the magistrates, who, as pagans, were held in low esteem by the Christians.

SEX, MARRIAGE, AND DIVORCE (Ch. 7). In order to understand Paul's pronouncements on these subjects, one should keep in mind three facts. First, himself a bachelor, he generally looked with disapproval upon sex relations. This is indicated not only in I Corinthians, but in several other places (e.g., Rom. 7:18 and Col. 3:5). Whereas Genesis 2:18 declares that "It is not good that the man should be alone," Paul asserts unequivocally that "It is good for a man not to touch a woman" (I Cor. 7:1) ("to touch a woman" was a euphemism for having sexual relations). For Paul the flesh is associated with sin, and fleshly impulses should be strictly curbed. Second, Corinth was noted as a city of libertinism and promiscuity, an environment of continual temptation for Christians. And, third, Paul believed that the Second Coming was to take place very soon.

Paul's views as expressed in I Corinthians might be summarized as follows: I wish that everybody were as I am—unmarried and uninterested in having sexual relations. But I am aware that most people are not like me. If one is not already married, I would advise him to remain single, for the Second Coming is so near that a Christian should devote all his time and energies to spiritual matters. It is better, however, to marry than to burn with sexual passion or to indulge in illicit sexual relations. If one *is* already married, let him not divorce his spouse.

EATING OF FOOD OFFERED TO PAGAN IDOLS (Chs. 8–10). Much of the meat available in the market places in Corinth came from animals sacrificed at pagan shrines.[4] Paul says that, inasmuch as no pagan worship was involved, there was no objection on his own part to eating such meat. He advises the Corinthian Christians, however, to respect the feelings of their fellows and to beware lest their own practices lead a weaker brother to do something against his conscience and therefore to sin. In Chapter 9, Paul re-enforces this argument by citing his own self-discipline and abnegation of rights for the sake of winning converts to the Gospel.

SOME MATTERS OF RITUAL (Ch. 11). Paul's "ordinance" that a woman cover her head during religious ceremonies (11:10-13) is apparently the origin of the requirement by some Christian sects today that women wear hats or veils in church.

In the latter part of Chapter 11, Paul gives his directions for Christianity's most holy and solemn rite—the Lord's Supper (Holy Communion, Eucharist, Holy Mass). His words are widely used in the service by many Protestant denominations today.

SPIRITUAL GIFTS AND LOVE (Chs. 12–14). Obviously, many of the members of the church at Corinth were failing to observe Jesus' teachings about humility and self-abnegation; for they were squabbling over which talents were the greatest—the ability to prophesy, to heal the sick, to perform miracles, to "talk in tongues" (engage in ecstatic utterance believed to be inspired by the Holy Spirit), and so on. Paul's answer is that all gifts and talents come from God, and all are therefore good. Just as every part of the body is necessary for its proper functioning, so the unselfish use of talents is necessary for the successful functioning of the Christian community, for all church members are parts of the body of Christ.

The late Professor Kirsopp Lake of Harvard said that he liked to imagine that at the end of the advice about talents, late at night Paul stopped composing his letter—weary from his labors, discouraged over the dissension in the Corinthian church, and rather sick at heart that those new converts had assimilated so little of the spirit of Christ's teachings. Then he went to bed. The next morning he arose refreshed and inspired with a simple answer to all the problems: If one is not motivated by loving kindness for his fellow man—love for one's neighbor such as the Good Samaritan showed—then all one's gifts and all one's endeavors are meaningless and worthless. The New Testament Greek word for this is *agapé*, translated variously as "love," "charity" (from the Latin *caritas*), and "sympathetic understanding."

This hymn to love (Ch. 13) has justly been considered one of the finest poetic passages in the Bible.

RESURRECTION AND PERSONAL IMMORTALITY (Ch. 15). Many Greeks believed in life after death, but they were inclined to think of it in terms of immortality of the spirit or mind or soul after its release from the body. The Hebrew view was that the soul could not exist without a body.

Now, some of the Corinthians apparently had denied the possibility of resurrection. This does not mean that they rejected belief in life after death, but that they doubted the existence of a *body* in the next world.

Paul accepted the Hebrew view. In this epistle, he first reviews for the Corinthians the experiences of many, including Peter and James, who had been eyewitnesses of Jesus' appearances in the flesh after the Resurrection. Then he points out that Christianity itself would be meaningless without belief in the immortality promised by Jesus and exemplified in his Resurrection. As for the sort of being who would exist in the afterlife, he admits that he does not know its exact nature. Flesh and blood, he says, can not inherit the kingdom of God, but in the hereafter the soul will be clothed in a new kind of body, a "spiritual body," or a "body of glory"—perhaps the sort of "body of glory" in which the spirit of Jesus made itself manifest to Paul himself on the road to Damascus at the time of his conversion to Christianity.

He ends the discussion with a rhapsodic hymn to life with Christ in the next world:

> For the trumpet shall sound,
> And the dead shall be raised incorruptible,
> And we shall be changed.
> For this corruptible must put on incorruption,
> And this mortal must put on immortality;
> So when this corruptible shall have put on incorruption,
> And this mortal shall have put on immortality,
> Then shall be brought to pass the saying that is written:
> Death is swallowed up in victory.
> O death, where is thy sting?
> O grave, where is thy victory? (15:52-58)

The Second Epistle to the Corinthians: The "Painful Letter" (Chs. 10–13). Although it is possible that the book called II Corinthians is one epistle reflecting two different moods, many scholars today feel that the tone of Chapters 10–13 is so drastically different from that of the first nine chapters that the two parts must be in fact two different letters; in the last four chapters Paul bitterly reproaches the Corinthians for their disloyalty to him, whereas Chapters 1–9 are filled with love, relief, and gratitude.[5] It seems likely that the reproachful letter was written before the conciliatory one, which, indeed, twice refers to an earlier, "painful" letter (2:3-9 and 7:8-12). The autobiographical value of both letters is very great, especially that of the former, which is a sort of *apologia pro vita sua*.

The mission of Timothy, bearing the letter now known as I Corinthians, seems to have met with no success; the party strife continued. Apparently Paul himself made a hurried second visit to Corinth (see II Cor. 12:14 and 13:1), which was also a failure. Now back at Ephesus, Paul writes a third letter, taking the Corinthians to task for doubting his apostolic authority and for following "false apostles"—presumably agents of the church at

Jerusalem—who "boasted" of their superior claims as Christian leaders.

REPROACH (10:1—13:10). Angry, hurt, and grieved, Paul asserts his own right to boast a little. He recounts the numerous hardships he has suffered for the cause of Christ—"in perils of waters, in perils of robbers, in perils by mine own countrymen, in perils by the heathen" (12:26); he has been beaten with rods and stoned; he has suffered shipwreck and a "thorn in the flesh" sent by Satan to "buffet" him (12:7).* Paul does not mention these matters to enlist the sympathies of the Corinthians, but to impress them with the fortitude which Christ gives him and to convince them of his loyalty to the Christian cause.

CONCLUSION (13:11-14). Once again he urges them to have done with quarreling, jealousy, selfishness, and disorder. He closes the epistle with the now famous benediction:

> The grace of the Lord Jesus Christ,
> And the love of God,
> And the communion of the Holy Ghost
> Be with you all. Amen. (13:14)

The Second Epistle to the Corinthians: The Letter of Reconciliation (1:1—6:13 and 7:2—9:15). The "painful" third letter must have accomplished its purpose, for the fourth is filled with gratitude and tenderness.

REJOICING AND RECONCILIATION (1:1—6:13, 7:2—8:24). Paul rejoices that his church has come back to him. He does not regret that his indignant letter has caused some of the Corinthians to grieve, because a "godly grief" leads to repentance, and repentance leads to salvation.

In a passage reminiscent of Jeremiah,† Paul tells how the Old Covenant (symbolized by the Ten Commandments on "tables of stone") has been superseded by the New Covenant preached by Christ, "written . . . with the Spirit of the living God . . . in fleshly tablets of the heart" (3:2-3).

Paul adds a note to his beliefs about the "spiritual body" as given in I Corthinians, Chapter 15. Whereas there he has taught

---

* See p. 82. Perhaps Dr. Luke, author of the third Gospel and of Acts, was later to serve as Paul's physician because of the ailment.
† See Jer. 31:31-33.

that the soul would be raised in a new body at the Last Judgment, now he holds that the spiritual body is already prepared and the soul will enter it at the time of death, when the "earthly house of this tabernacle" is dissolved. Then the soul will begin a new life, which is everlasting (5:1-10). Paul emphasizes also the spiritual nature of Christian life from the time of conversion (5:16-17).

APPEAL FOR CONTRIBUTIONS (Chs. 8–9). At the end of this letter, Paul once again shows his practical side: he asks the Corinthians for contributions of money for the church at Jerusalem. He urges them to give generously and willingly, for "God loveth a cheerful giver" (9:7). After some rather commonplace arguments for liberality, he abruptly ends his appeal: "Thanks be to God for his unspeakable gift"—as if to say, "If gratitude to God for the gift of his Son does not move you to give, then nothing can motivate your giving!" [6]

THE EPISTLE TO THE GALATIANS: "THE CHRISTIAN DECLARATION OF INDEPENDENCE"

Though a relatively short letter, the Epistle to the Galatians is a highly important Christian document. It is important for two reasons: first, it contains some primary autobiographical and historical material; and, second, it marks the parting of the ways between Judaism and Christianity.

Although some of the reasoning in the letter may be unconvincing and perhaps distasteful to a modern reader, the fervor and sincerity with which it was written make it also valuable as a piece of literature.

There is much uncertainty as to the date and place of composition and even as to its addressees.[7] It seems likely, however, that it was written at Ephesus in A.D. 53 or 54 and that it was addressed to the churches in southern Asia Minor, in the Roman province known as Galatia—probably such churches as those at Derbe, Lystra, and Iconium founded by Paul on his first missionary journey among the Gentiles.

The occasion for the writing of the epistle is clear enough. Certain elements in the church at Jerusalem still regarded Paul with distrust, probably because he had formerly led in persecution of the Christians; and some, the "circumcision" party, still held that a would-be convert had to accept Judaism before becoming a Christian. Hence they had sent missionaries to Galatia to discredit Paul and his doctrines. Paul's letter is a defense of (1) his own credentials as an Apostle and (2) his conception of Christianity as a totally new religion, "a world religion instead of a Jewish sect." [8]

Paul's Claims to Apostolic Authority (Chs. 1–2). The letter opens not with the conventional salutation, but with Paul's claim to his title as an Apostle—"not of men, neither by man, but by Jesus Christ, and God the Father, who raised him from the dead." He has received his appointment from God himself, who revealed his Son directly to him on the way to Damascus. Thereafter he has been accepted by Peter, John, and James the brother of Jesus, who all gave him the "right hands of fellowship" and who at the Jerusalem Council (see p. 86) recognized his commitment as a missionary to the Gentiles.

Justification by Faith (Chs. 3–4). Chapters 3 and 4 expound succinctly Paul's doctrine of justification by faith alone, a doctrine later elaborated in the Epistle to the Romans. Paul argues that, whereas men have failed to attain righteousness by obeying the Hebrew Law, God has granted them salvation if they will have faith in Jesus Christ and his Gospel. Abraham was "justified" by faith, and God made a covenant with him and his descendants; but when these descendants sinned, the Law was added to control them—a necessary but temporary expedient. Now that Christ has come to reveal the Gospel, the Law is not only unnecessary but also a "curse," a bondage from which the Gospel frees man by making him a son and heir of God rather than a servant.

The "Fruit of the Spirit" (5:1—6:10). Paul explains that the new freedom of the Gospel is not a license to live immorally. If one has true faith, then he will "walk in the Spirit" and not "fulfil the lust of the flesh." The works of the flesh are wicked— adultery, idolatry, wrath, drunkenness, murders, and many others; but the "fruit of the Spirit is love, peace, longsuffering, gentleness, goodness, faith, meekness, temperance" (5:22-23). Paul urges his addressees to "Bear ye one another's burdens, and so fulfil the law of Christ" (6:2) and to "not be weary in well doing" (6:9); and he warns: "Be not deceived; God is not mocked: for whatsoever a man soweth, that shall he also reap" (6:7).

Conclusion (6:11-18). Paul recapitulates his main points in a postscript written in "large" letters by his own hand.

THE EPISTLE TO THE ROMANS: A TREATISE ON
FAITH AND ELECTION

After completing his third missionary journey (probably A.D. 56, though possibly 55 or 57), Paul returned to Corinth to await passage to Judea for the delivering of the money he had collected for the "saints in Jerusalem" (see discussion of the Corinthian letters above). He seized the opportunity afforded by this period of relative leisure to write to the Christian community at Rome, a church which he himself had not founded and whose members he did not know.

Purposes. Several circumstances may have prompted him to write to this church. (1) Believing himself under God's mandate to carry the Gospel to all Gentile nations (1:5), he had long been contemplating a missionary journey to Rome on the way to Spain, and this letter would introduce him to the Roman Christians and so help prepare for his reception in the capital city. (2) A clear statement of his theological views was needed to combat any hostility against him which might have been aroused by the Judaizing party of the church. And (3) Rome, the hub of the Empire, was the best place for preserving his doctrines and disseminating them over all the known world; hence in this letter he gives a careful and systematic summary of some of his basic views.

Style and Organization. Composed at leisure, perhaps over a period of two or three months, and addressed to an unfamiliar audience on whom Paul wanted to make a good impression, the Epistle to the Romans is far more systematically planned and carefully written than most of Paul's letters. Generally it is calmer, more objective, and more impersonal than his earlier writings. Some of the close reasoning leaves us unmoved today, but some passages (such as 8:38-39, quoted p. 124) are filled with Paul's usual enthusiasm. It is not a letter intended to quell local controversies or to solve personal disputes, like I Corinthians or Galatians. Instead, it is a relatively serene document which lays the foundation for a large part of later Christian theology, or, as one commentator puts it, "All roads lead to Romans."

Justification by Faith (Chs. 1–8). The first section is an elaboration of the views Paul expressed in his letter to the Galatians (see above). Faith and faith alone, he says, will lead to salvation. The Gentiles have tried wisdom, but this has led to corruption; the Hebrews have relied on their Law, but this has been found insufficient. The Law has distinguished between good and evil, but has provided no satisfactory motivation or power towards righteousness. From the beginning, God intended faith in him as the only means to salvation; he gave the Hebrews the Law only as a temporary set of rules till Jesus Christ could bring the Good News—the truth about God's love and his promise of eternal life. Faith sets a man free from the Law, not by giving him license, but by making an entirely new creature of him, an unselfish being who performs God's will eagerly and joyously. This New Man has found a new sort of freedom, happiness, and peace; for nothing can destroy his eternal relationship with God:

> For I am persuaded, that neither death, nor life, nor angels, nor principalities, nor powers, nor things present, nor things to come, nor height, nor depth, nor any other creature, shall be able to separate us from the love of God, which is in Christ Jesus our Lord. (8:38-39) °

This blessed state—salvation or "justification"—is not something that we can earn or deserve, but a free gift from God. In order to obtain it, all we need to do is to have faith, and there is no other way.

The Destiny of Israel (Chs. 9–11). The second section of Romans sounds like a rebuttal to those who might argue that God has broken his promise to the Hebrews. Most of them have rejected Christianity; therefore they will not be saved. Yet God long ago promised to regard them as his Chosen People. How can these two beliefs be reconciled? Paul answers that God is carrying out his promise in glorious though inscrutable ways. At the beginning of time God chose his "elect," those who would be "saved," but these are the people who place their faith in Jesus Christ and his Gospel.†

Moral Exhortations (Chs. 12–13). Fearing, perhaps, that his doctrines concerning freedom from the Law might lead to what was later termed Antinomianism (that is, the doctrine that a

---

° Compare Socrates' dictum, as quoted by Plato in the *Apology:* "No evil can happen to a good man, either in life or after death."

† For nearly two millennia theologians have argued over whether these statements of Paul are an endorsement of predestination and a denial of the freedom of the will. See also the discussion of the Epistle to the Ephesians below.

Christian is exempt from moral law), Paul devoted the third part of his letter to a series of precepts for personal and social behavior: love your brothers, pray regularly, be patient in tribulation, be generous and hospitable, live in harmony with one another, leave vengeance to the Lord, "Be not be overcome of evil, but overcome evil with good" (12:21). Especially noteworthy is Paul's advice to the Roman Christians that they obey the governing authorities (13:1-7). Having always shown great respect for the Roman government as the maintainer of peace and order in the world, he argues here that civil obedience is not only expedient but also in accord with God's will.

Covering Letter (Ch. 16). Chapter 16 is believed by some scholars to be a "covering" letter addressed to various individuals known to be in Ephesus, and later by mistake attached to the Epistle to the Romans. It exhorts the brethren to avoid dissension. Both this letter and Chapter 15 end with benedictions.

THE "CAPTIVITY" LETTERS

Internal evidence indicates that Paul wrote the epistles to the Colossians, to Philemon, to the Ephesians, and to the Philippians while he was imprisoned (Col. 4:2-3, 18; Philemon 1,9; and Phil. 1:7,13). In none of these passages, however, does he mention *where* he is imprisoned. It has been traditional to assume that the place was Rome and that the date, therefore, was about A.D. 60 or 61. Some modern scholars have argued that the imprisonment was that at Caesarea (see Acts 23:23—26:32) or one which he suffered at Ephesus but which is not mentioned in Acts. These arguments, however, are unconvincing, and there seems to be little reason to abandon the traditional assumption that the letters were written in Rome.[9] All were intrusted for delivery, it appears, to the messenger Tychicus (see Col. 4:7 and Eph. 6:21-22).

The Epistle to the Colossians: Paul's First Attack on "Heresy." Colossae was a small city in the Roman province of Asia, about a hundred miles east of Ephesus. Paul's missionary journeys had not taken him to the region, but he was deeply interested in the Christian churches, apparently established by Epaphras, in Colossae and in the nearby cities of Laodicea and Hierapolis.

The occasion for the writing of the letter to the Colossians was a visit by Epaphras to Paul in prison. He needed Paul's help in combatting a dangerous doctrine which threatened what he considered the "orthodox" Christian faith in Colossae. This doctrine (a forerunner of the second-century movement known as Gnosticism) was a combination of Jewish and pagan elements: faith in Christ was supplemented by a belief in certain cosmic powers (perhaps angelic spirits) which were thought to govern the physical and material world and to require propitiation by various rites and magical observances. Details of the heretical "philosophy" are lacking; our knowledge must be inferred from Paul's criticism. Unfortunately, many of his phrases, though undoubtedly clear to his addressees, are obscure to us.

THE ABSOLUTE SUPREMACY OF CHRIST (1:1—4:6). Quickly perceiving the danger that Christ might be reduced to the level of *e pluribus unum* or "just one more" of the cosmic powers, Paul vigorously asserts his supremacy and his identity with God the Creator:

[He] is the image of the invisible God, the firstborn of every creature: For by him were all things created, that are in heaven, and that are in earth, visible and invisible . . . (1:15-16)

Here for the first time in his letters Paul identifies Jesus with the Logos, an identification which was later to play a significant part in Christian theology.* He asserts, further, that Christ does not share his work of redemption and salvation with any of the powers of the universe; faith in him alone is sufficient for man, whom he has redeemed by his death on the Cross. Man does not need other mediators, nor should he fear and worship spirits. Salvation lies in putting on the new life as taught by Jesus, a life "where there is neither Greek nor Jew, circumcision nor uncircumcision, Barbarian, Scythian, bond nor free: but Christ is all, and in all" (3:11).

CONCLUSION (4:7-18). As was his custom, Paul ends his epistle with some advice to members of the church at Colossae and some personal greetings to several individuals.

The Epistle to Philemon: An Appeal for a Runaway Slave. The brief but charming composition known as the Epistle to Philemon † is concerned with the treatment of Onesimus (mentioned also in Col. 4:9), a slave who has apparently stolen money

* See the discussion of the Logos in connection with the Gospel of John, above, pp. 102-103.

† The epistle is addressed to three members of the church at Colossae: Philemon, Apphia, and Archippus (probably members of one household,

from his owner, run away and joined Paul (presumably in Rome), and been converted to Christianity.

PURPOSE. At first blush, the letter seems to be primarily an appeal to the master to treat Onesimus mercifully upon his return. More careful reading suggests that perhaps its purpose (expressed in a hint in verses 13 and 21: "whom I would have retained with me, that in thy stead he might have ministered unto me . . ." and "knowing that thou wilt do more than I say") is to persuade the owner to free Onesimus so that he may return to Paul.[10]

HISTORICAL SIGNIFICANCE. This letter is historically important for its treatment of slavery in the Roman world, where the slave was considered only a chattel of the master, who was free to subject him to any sort of servitude and who could condemn him to death by crucifixion or stoning if he was recaptured after running away. Paul has often been censured for failing to attack the whole system, but such an attack not only would have been futile, but also might have caused the Christians to be branded as a subversive sect. Furthermore, Paul's exhortations to the slave to be docile and patient and to the master to be lenient and understanding probably were more effective in easing the lot of the slaves than would have been any attack on a system which obtained over the entire Roman Empire; and he *did* urge Onesimus' master to take him back not as a slave but as "a brother beloved, specially to me, but how much more unto thee, both in the flesh, and in the Lord" (v.16).

STYLE. This is the only purely *personal* letter which has survived out of the numerous ones which Paul must surely have written. It is especially valuable, therefore, for its revelation of its author's personality, which his acquaintances everywhere obviously found gracious, lovable, and persuasive. "It is one of the most charming letters ever written—full of kindness and the finest courtesy, with delicate touches of pathos and also of playfulness." [11]

---

where a Christian group met). It and the Epistle to the Colossians were apparently dispatched at the same time. Traditionally, Philemon has been considered the owner of the slave Onesimus. But Albert Barnett, in *The New Testament: Its Making and Meaning*, rev. ed. (Nashville: Abingdon Press, 1958), p. 88, argues that Philemon was the minister of the church at Colossae and that Archippus was Onesimus' master.

The Epistle to the Ephesians: A Treatise on the Purpose of Christ and the Church. The group to whom the third of the "Captivity" epistles is addressed is unknown. According to the first verse as it now stands, the letter was directed to "the saints who are in Ephesus," but several ancient manuscripts lack the last phrase. Perhaps it was intended as a circular letter to be read to several church congregations, and therefore the author left a blank, to be filled in by the messenger as he read the letter to each church; or perhaps this is the "lost" letter to the church at Laodicea (mentioned in Col. 4:16). In the second century, Marcion labeled it "Epistle to the Laodiceans." At any rate, most scholars agree that it was not written for the Ephesian Christians, among whom Paul had spent much time during the preceding three years; it contains no personal greetings and appears to be addressed to an audience with whom the author was unfamiliar.

AUTHORSHIP. But was the author Paul? There is much scholarly disagreement here. Differences in style and in attitude toward the "saints and apostles" between this letter and the clearly authentic Pauline writings have led many commentators, especially American and German ones, to assign this epistle to some disciple of Paul. Inasmuch as the matter is still unresolved, let us follow the traditional view that Paul is the author.[12]

STYLE. Not occasioned by any emergency or dissension or heresy arising in one of the young churches, the Epistle to the Ephesians has a tone of serenity, of quiet joy; it has a prayerlike quality, and, indeed, many prayers are scattered throughout the six chapters. It might appropriately be called a religious meditation.[13]

GOD'S PURPOSE (Chs. 1–3). The theological content of Ephesians is much the same as that of Colossians, but here there is no need to inveigh against any theological doctrine. With calm assurance, Paul makes the following points:

From the beginning, God intended that men should live in love and harmony with each other and in obedience to him. Something happened, however, to set men at strife with each other and to alienate them from God. Now redemption and the promise of unity have come through the life, death, and Resurrection of Jesus Christ: "Having made known unto us the mystery of his will, according to his good pleasure which he hath purposed in himself; That in the dispensation of the fulness of times he might gather together in one all things in Christ, both which are in heaven, and which are on earth; even in him" (1:9-10). Paul emphasizes that the role of Christ, who is coeternal with the Father, is part of God's original plan. The first three chapters of Ephesians elaborate on these points.

THE CHURCH AS THE BODY OF CHRIST (Chs. 3-6). In the second half of the letter Paul develops the idea that the church, which is the body of Christ, is God's instrument of reconciliation, by which all men, Jews as well as Gentiles, will be brought back into harmony with one another and with God. Largely hortatory, this portion of the letter gives practical advice as to how Christians must aid in carrying out God's great plans for reconciliation. Paul concludes the letter with a benediction.

The Epistle to the Philippians: A Letter of Assurance and Joy. If the assumption that the Captivity letters were written in Rome is correct, it may well be that the Epistle to the Philippians was Paul's last composition. It is addressed to the Christian community at Philippi, the church for which the Apostle seems to have had the most affection—his "brethren dearly beloved and longed for," his "joy and crown" (4:1).

PURPOSE. The occasion for its writing was the purposed return to Philippi of Epaphroditus, who had brought Paul a gift of money from the Philippian church and who had intended to remain a long while as his companion during the imprisonment. But Epaphroditus had suffered a serious illness, which left him with a great yearning to return to his own city. Now Paul sends him on his way bearing this letter.

STYLE. The tone of the Epistle to the Philippians is somewhat autumnal and serene, like the Epistle to the Ephesians. Both seem the utterances of an aging man who has learned forbearance and found peace: "I have learned, in whatsoever state I am, therewith to be content" (Phil. 4:11). But the Philippian letter is full of surety, of confidence, and of joy; indeed, in its four short chapters the word *joy* appears five times and *rejoice*, nine times. What a triumphant farewell to life from a man who had kept the faith and finished the course: "Rejoice in the Lord alway: and again I say, Rejoice"! (4:4).

SALUTATION AND PERSONAL MESSAGES. (Chs. 1-3). After a brief greeting and benediction to "all the saints in Christ Jesus which are at Philippi," Paul pours out his gratitude to them for their

partnership in spreading the Gospel and for their steadfastness
in the faith. Eager to dispel their gloom caused by his imprisonment, he hints that he may soon be free to visit them, and he
assures them that meanwhile his lot is far from being unbearable.
Even if things should become much worse, his trust in his Master
would keep him brave and happy. Whether he is to live or to die
makes little difference: "For me to live is Christ and to die is
gain" (1:21).

COMFORT AND EXHORTATION (Ch. 3). Paul sympathizes with
the Philippians over hardships which they have been suffering
(apparently some dissensions within the membership and some
persecution at the hands of the Judaists), but he assures them
that all these difficulties will pass away if they persevere in the
Christian faith and way of life.* He exhorts them to be unselfish,
humble, and uncomplaining. Nothing is really important except
devotion to Christ: "But what things were gain to me, those I
counted loss for Christ. Yea doubtless, and I count all things but
loss for the excellency of the knowledge of Christ Jesus my Lord
. . ." (3:7-8).

CONCLUSION (Ch. 4). Paul ends the letter with more personal
messages, expressions of appreciation, and a benediction.

---

* A bitter passage (3:2-21) concerning enemies who have been trying to
undermine his work in Philippi is thought by some scholars to be a fragment
of another letter which somehow has been interpolated into the text.

8

The Epistle to the Hebrews:
A Sermon on Faith

Although for many centuries the magnificent oration known as the Epistle to the Hebrews was attributed to Paul, there is now almost unanimous agreement that he was not its author. Whereas Paul's "impassioned utterances read like inspired impromptus," [1] this is the product of a writer who is conscious of himself as a literary artist; who takes great pains with matters of diction, style, and rhetoric; and who carefully organizes his material so as to build to a tremendous climax (in the famous "faith" passage, Chapter 11). Further evidences that Paul did not write it are the author's scant knowledge of Judaism, his totally un-Pauline conception of "salvation," and his atttiude toward Hebrew Law. Many Biblical scholars have tried to identify the author and have nominated Barnabas, Clement of Rome, Priscilla (mentioned in Rom. 16:3, I Cor. 16:19, II Tim. 4:19), and Apollos. The last-named, who is described in Acts 18:24 as "born at Alexandria, an eloquent man, . . . mighty in the scriptures," seems the most likely candidate; but most modern scholars are inclined to agree with the third-century Origen, who said, "The author is known to God alone."

DATE, PLACE, AND STYLE

The date of composition is uncertain. A work attributed to Clement of Rome (A.D. 96) quotes from it, but Clement's authorship has been questioned. References in Hebrews to a tabernacle set up by Moses have been thought to mean the Temple in Jerusalem, in which case the work would probably have to be dated before A.D. 70, when the Temple was destroyed, since there is no reference to this event. However, the allusions may not be to that Temple. The "letter" reflects (1) a time of persecution of the Christians and (2) Christian attitudes of the last part of the century. A likely date is A.D. 80-90.[2]

Both the destination and the place of composition are disputable. The title "To the Hebrews" is very old (used by Tertullian early in the third century), but the contents appear to be addressed simply to discouraged and backsliding Christians, with no distinction made between Gentiles and Jewish converts. The closing greeting (13:24) is ambiguous: "They of Italy salute you." The Greek, as well as the English, could mean "those *in* Italy" or "those *who come from* Italy." [3] A fair guess is that the work was written in Rome to some unidentified Christian community outside of Italy.

Finally, there is the question of whether Hebrews is an epistle. It closes with the usual epistolary greetings and personal messages, but it begins like an address rather than a letter; there is no formal salutation. Furthermore, the style is eloquent and oratorical. It has been suggested that the first part of the scroll, containing the initial salutation, has been lost; but what seems more likely is that the author wrote a speech to be read to an audience and closed it with the customary personal remembrances.[4]

PURPOSE AND MESSAGE

The purpose of the sermon (if such it be), like that of Daniel and Revelation, is to encourage a group suffering for its religion to hold on to its faith. It refers to an earlier period of afflictions (perhaps the persecution by Nero in A.D. 64-65) and exhorts its audience to remain steadfast in this one (perhaps the persecution by Domitian in A.D. 81-96). But the danger appears to be not so much from fear on the part of the addressees as from indifference and lethargy. This has led some scholars to believe that the references are not to specific persecutions but to general conditions. Theirs, the author says, is the only true religion, a fulfillment of the promise inherent in Judaism. God's purpose from the beginning has been to manifest himself to man so that man will worship him truly. Glimpses of that purpose were caught and held by faith by some of the Old Testament patriarchs, prophets, and other religious leaders. Now the manifestation has been accomplished fully in the person of Jesus Christ, the High Priest who shares man's humanity but is without sin. Christ is able to bring direct communion and reconciliation with God. He is the personification of God's Word,* and God's purpose will be completed at the Second Coming, which will take place soon. The hearers (or readers) are urged to renew their enthusiasm and to cling to their faith.

* Compare the Gospel of John (see pp. 102-103), where the doctrine of the Logos is elaborated.

9

The Pastoral Epistles

From the second to the eighteenth century three letters—I and II Timothy and Titus—were attributed to Paul, but they are now believed by most scholars to be the products of one of Paul's disciples. They are all indisputably by the same author; but matters of style, vocabulary, theology, and reflection of church organization all indicate that Paul was not the author.[1] Some fragments seem to have been written by Paul himself, preserved for several decades by one of his followers, and then incorporated into letters of advice to pastors of young churches. Hence the letters have come to be known as the Pastoral Epistles. The date of composition is uncertain; some scholars suggest as early as A.D. 100; others, as late as 140.[2] They are ostensibly addressed to Timothy and Titus, Paul's missionary companions mentioned so often in Acts and in the Pauline letters. Perhaps they symbolized to the author the younger clergy of his own day.

The literary value of the Pastoral letters is considerably lower than that of the genuine Pauline epistles. The style is prolix, and the sentence structure is loose and monotonous. The warmth and vigor which we find in Galatians and Corinthians, for example, are lacking. Of the 848 different words (not counting proper names) in the Pastorals, 306 are found only in these three epistles, and they belong to the vocabulary of the second Christian century.[3]

Historically, the Pastoral Epistles are significant for two reasons. First, they reveal the changes in church organization from the era when the early missionaries traveled about, making converts and organizing them into small communities of brethren, to the time when local control passed into the hands of the community pastors and when "bishops," "elders," and "deacons" had clearly prescribed functions. And, second, they throw light on the growth of syncretistic "heresies" within the second-century church.

The theological content of these epistles is basically Pauline, but the author lacks Paul's fervor and spiritual insight. For him, faith means formal acceptance of Christian dogma; "outward performance" is regarded as more important than "inward fellowship with Christ," and the Holy Spirit seems to be more a power granted to ecclesiastical officials than a force working within each individual.[4]

THE FIRST EPISTLE TO TIMOTHY: FALSE LEADERS AND ECCLESIASTICAL DUTIES

The first Pastoral, addressed to Timothy in Ephesus, has two purposes: (1) to oppose the speculative mythology of Gnosticism —"profane and old wives' tales" (4:7), which spread false teachings about the Gospel; and (2) to outline the qualifications and duties of "bishops" and "deacons," with particular emphasis on how these church leaders can combat the false teachings.

This epistle is especially interesting for its references to the various members of the Christian community—widows and young women, slaves and masters, young men and old, bishops and deacons. It also contains some practical (and now proverbial) advice: "Drink no longer water, but use a little wine for thy stomach's sake and thine often infirmities" (5:23) and "the love of money is the root of all evil" (6:10).

THE SECOND EPISTLE TO TIMOTHY: QUALITIES OF A GOOD PREACHER

The second Epistle to Timothy is more personal and intimate than the first. The author longs to see the addressee again and recalls affectionately Timothy's mother Eunice and grandmother Lois. After mentioning his own experiences as a missionary, he tells his young colleague that fortitude is the most important quality of a preacher. Also important is the avoidance of "false teaching," of disputation and "godless chatter," and of godless people—the selfish, the proud, the treacherous, the unholy, and the chasers after pleasure.

Some scholars believe that most famous passage in the letter *sounds* like Paul and may include a genuine fragment from one of his notes written as he calmly faced execution in Rome: "For I am ready to be offered, and the time of my departure is at hand. I have fought a good fight, I have finished my course [race], I have kept the faith: Henceforth there is laid up for me a crown of righteousness, which the Lord, the righteous judge, shall give me at that day . . ." (4:6-8).

THE EPISTLE TO TITUS: ADVICE TO BISHOPS
AND PREACHERS

The letter to Titus (in Crete) is little more than a repetition of the advice given in I Timothy. It may well be that the two epistles were dispatched simultaneously to the two disciples of the author, carrying counsel concerning the problems which seemed most pressing at the moment.

A bishop, the letter says, must be the husband of only one wife; he must be the blameless steward of God; and he must be hospitable, sober, just, holy, and temperate.

Again the author warns against false teachings, "Jewish fables, and commandments of men, that turn from the truth" (1:14). He instructs Titus in the qualities which the various members of the church should cultivate (compare I Tim. 5–6). He cautions all Christians to avoid speaking evil of others, brawling, foolish bickering about the Law, thievery, ungodliness, and worldly lusts—so that they may look forward to Christ's Second Coming, "that blessed hope, and the glorious appearing of the great God and our Saviour Jesus Christ" (2:13).

10

The General (or Catholic) Epistles

From three to seven writings are usually classed together as the "General" or "Catholic" Epistles because they apparently were directed to several communities or to the Christian church at large rather than to any one person or congregation. To consider them as a unified group is a mistake, for each letter has its own individual purpose and message. Scholars have differed about which epistles are "general"; most of them agree on James, II Peter, and I John; some include also one or more of the following: I Peter, Jude, II John, and III John.

THE FIRST EPISTLE OF PETER: A NOTE OF HOPE DURING A PERIOD OF PERSECUTION

The document known as the First Epistle of Peter is now believed to be an anonymous encyclical (circular letter) addressed to the churches in Pontus, Galatia, Cappadocia, Asia, and Bythinia (1:1)—all in the northern half of Asia Minor.

Though of relatively small value as a source of doctrine, the First Epistle of Peter "is one of the most beautiful writings in the New Testament, not philosophical or profound, but full of the purest spirit of devotion." [1]

Authorship. Although it has been traditionally assigned to the Apostle Peter, for three reasons it is most unlikely that he was the author: (1) the Greek in which it is written is too correct and elegant to be the product of a Galilean fisherman; (2) the epistle is saturated with Pauline doctrine which would have been both unknown and unacceptable to Peter; and (3) its probable date is too late for Peter, especially if one credits the tradition that that Apostle was martyred about A.D. 65. The letter appears to have been written in Rome and addressed to all Christians—both

Jewish converts and Gentile—of the communities named above.

Date and Purpose. The epistle's date and its purpose must be considered together. In a time of general persecution of Christians, it was written to bring hope and comfort to the sufferers and to exhort them to persevere in the faith and live blameless lives. The persecution reflected is more universal and continuous than any mentioned in Acts or than the Neronian massacre of the seventh decade of the century; it appears to be a later persecution, occurring some time between A.D. 80 and 96. The letter was probably written during these sixteen years.

The content of the epistle is almost entirely hortatory. The author tells his addresses that they are not alone in their sufferings; other churches are aware of their hardships and are suffering similarly. These hardships are intended as a test of their faith. They are reminded of Christ's sufferings in their behalf and of his patience. The terrible period of persecution will soon pass, and the faithful will enter a period of great peace and happiness.

The Descent into Hell. Two unusually interesting passages deal with Jesus' descent into hell, presumably during the period between the Crucifixion and the Resurrection:

[He was] put to death in the flesh, but quickened by the Spirit: By which also he went and preached unto the spirits in prison; Which sometime were disobedient, when once the longsuffering of God waited in the days of Noah, . . . For for this cause was the gospel preached also to them that are dead, that they might be judged according to men in the flesh, but live according to God in the spirit. (3:18-20 and 4:6)

These passages are the origin of the phrase, preserved in the Apostles' Creed, "He descended into hell," and of the medieval tradition of the "Harrowing of Hell"—the belief that Jesus journeyed through the world of the dead and rescued therefrom all the virtuous who had died before they could be saved by his Gospel.

THE EPISTLE OF JAMES: A PLEA FOR "GOOD WORKS"

This letter is addressed to "the twelve tribes which are scattered abroad"—that is, of the Dispersion. The phrase "twelve tribes" apparently refers not to the ancient tribes of Israel (for they had ceased to exist as entities several centuries earlier), but rather to the various Christian communities all over the Mediterranean world, which now considered themselves the "new Israel."

Authorship, Date, and Place. The opening words attribute the letter to "James, a servant of God and of the Lord Jesus Christ." It has been traditional to identify the author with James the brother of Jesus; but James was a common name then as now, and most scholars consider the author to be some Christian teacher named James, otherwise unidentifiable.

The date and place of composition are also unknown.[2] Apparent acquaintance with the Gospels of Matthew and Luke, and what seems to be an attack on Paul's doctrine of justification by faith indicate a date at the very end of the first century, say A.D. 96-100. The author's familiarity with the Greek language and Greek modes of thought is evidence that he lived in some Gentile region; Rome has been suggested as most likely.

Purpose. The principal purpose of the letter is to convince its readers that "faith without works is dead" (2:26). It is clear that the author interprets "faith" to be mere intellectual assent to Jesus' Messiahship and to the truth of his teachings. James seems not to realize Paul's conviction that acceptance of Jesus and the Gospel is irresistibly compelling motivation to do good "works." The very example that Paul chose as an illustration of salvation by faith (Rom. 4:1-22) James uses as an illustration of salvation by *doing* good deeds: "Was not Abraham our father justified by works, when he had offered Isaac his son upon the altar? Seest thou how faith wrought with his works, and by works was faith made perfect?" (2:21-22).*

Spirit, Style, and Contents. The Epistle of James is similar in spirit, style, and content to several other Biblical books. It is similar in spirit and content to some of the Old Testament prophets, notably Amos, Isaiah, and Micah, in their stern condemnation of those who give lip service to God but who fail to perform righteous deeds. It resembles these same eighth-century B.C. prophets and also the Synoptic Gospels in its denunciation of the rich (and perhaps of riches themselves):

But ye have despised the poor. Do not rich men oppress you, and draw you before the judgment seats? Do not they blaspheme that worthy name by the which ye are called? . . . Go to now, ye rich men,

---

* See, for example, Eph. 4–6 and Col. 3–4.

weep and howl for your miseries that shall come upon you. Your riches are corrupted and your garments motheaten. Your gold and silver is cankered; and the rust of them shall be a witness against you, and shall eat your flesh as it were fire. Ye have heaped treasure together for the last days.* (2:6-7 and 5:1-3)

In form and style the epistle sounds like a combination of the Epistle to the Hebrews and the Book of Proverbs, for it is a sermon filled with practical precepts for daily living (notice especially Chapter 3, on "taming the tongue"). It is memorable for its fifty-four imperatives (in 108 verses), its irony, its humor, and its vigor.

THE EPISTLES OF JOHN

Through the centuries Christian tradition has attributed to the Apostle John the authorship of the fourth Gospel, the book of Revelation, and the three epistles of John. Though there is still some disagreement, the majority of modern scholars hold the following views: (1) The Apostle John did not write any of the five books. (2) Matters of theology, style, and diction indicate that one author, unidentifiable, wrote the Gospel and the three letters, but *not* Revelation.[3] The letters were probably written at Ephesus during the period A.D. 100-110.

The First Epistle of John: A Defense of the Christian Doctrine. Though sometimes classed as a General Epistle, I John might more properly be described as a tract or a sermon, for it has no customary epistolary salutation or benediction. It appears to be addressed to a group of churches in Asia Minor.

The author's simple and artless characterization of God and his harmonious blending of the mystical and the practical make this brief letter not only a beautiful piece of literature but also an important Christian document.

PURPOSE. The principal purpose of the letter is to combat the heresy known as Docetism, by setting forth the "truth" about the nature of Jesus Christ. The Docetists ("Seemists"), were a branch of Gnostics (see p. 99), who denied that Christ could be at once divine and human. They held that salvation lay in the *knowledge* (*gnosis*) of divine mysteries. Those who possessed such knowledge were incapable of sin and therefore free of any moral obligations—a doctrine called *Antinomianism,* perhaps a distortion of Paul's doctrine of justification by faith.

---

* Compare Amos 4:1-2; Micah 2:1—3:3; and Matt. 6:19-21 and 19:16-24.

CONTENTS. Without attempting a logical, point-by-point refutation, the author of I John warns against the "false teachers" of these heretical beliefs and argues that true religion is a matter of the soul's relationship to God and its communion with him. He offers three tests of the validity of one's religious experience: [4] (1) The test of ethical conduct; if we *know* God, we will keep his commandments (2:3). (2) The test of belief; if we believe that Jesus is the incarnation of God's spirit, then that Spirit will dwell in our hearts and lead us to the truth (4:2-3). (3) The test of brotherly love (which the Docetists felt irrelevant):

Beloved, let us love one another: for love is of God; and everyone that loveth is born of God and knoweth God. He that loveth not knoweth not God; for God is love. . . . If a man say, I love God, and hateth his brother, he is a liar: for he that loveth not his brother whom he hath seen, how can he love God whom he hath not seen? (4:7-8, 20)

John's main point (reminiscent of Paul's doctrine in I Cor. 13) is that since it is God's nature to love, then man also must be filled with that same spirit as the motive force for all his actions; otherwise he is not a true Christian.

The Second Epistle of John: A Plea for Orthodoxy. This short letter (thirteen verses) is addressed by "the elder" to an "elect lady and her children." It is quite evident that the "lady" is some church dear to the author's heart.

In much the same tone as in I John, the author warns the congregation against the "deceiver" and "antichrist"—apparently those propagating Docetism and Antinomianism, false teachers who deny that "Jesus Christ is come in the flesh" (v. 7). He rejoices that some members are living the true life and enjoins them not to receive any of the "progressive" teachers.

He concludes his letter with greetings and a hope to visit the "lady" soon.

The Third Epistle of John: An Attack on a Rival. John's third letter is addressed to one Gaius, seemingly a man of some importance. The author commends him on showing hospitality to certain missionaries, but beseeches him not to extend such hospitality to Diotrephes, for that ambitious leader has spread false rumors about the "elder" (the author) and has tried to have excommunicated those who want to welcome "the brethren."

The brief letter (fourteen verses) is historically significant for reflecting a change in church organization.* Formerly, an itinerant missionary, under the direction of an Apostle, had been enthusiastically and reverently received by a congregation, governed by a board of elders. Now a missionary was finding difficulty in being received at all. Leadership was beginning to pass into the hands of a local, permanent ruler ("bishop"), who not only might refuse hospitality to missionaries, but also could assume the power of excommunicating any member who refused him obedience. Thus the era of the itinerant missionary was nearing an end; each church was able to stand by itself.

THE EPISTLE OF JUDE: ANOTHER POLEMIC
AGAINST THE GNOSTIC HERESY

The author of this short letter describes himself as "the servant of Jesus Christ, and brother of James." That he was neither the one of the Twelve Disciplines known as "Judas, the son [or brother] of James" (Luke 6:16) nor Judas, the brother of James and Jesus, seems evidenced by his failure to claim apostleship and by his reference to the Apostles as belonging to the rather distant past (vss. 17-18). Jude (or Judas) was a very common Jewish name, and most modern commentators consider the author unidentifiable.

Date and Contents. The implications that the Apostolic Age had long been over, the attack on heretics (vss. 4-21), and the reference to the Christian faith as something very old, "delivered to the saints" (v. 3)—all these indicate a date in the second century. The period 125-150 seems likely.[5] Apparently written in Rome [6] and addressed to Christians everywhere—"to those who are sanctified by God the Father, and preserved in Jesus Christ" (v. 1), the letter is an attack on Gnostic doctrine and Antinomian immorality. Citing from the Old Testament and from Hebrew apocolypses many examples of the terrible punishment which has fallen upon scoffers and evildoers, the author excoriates those who deny Christ as the Master (vss. 3-4) and who have fallen into sins of self-indulgence—an immorality which "is the natural corollary of their heresy." [7] The Apostles of old, he says, warned that there would be "mockers in the last time" (a reflection of his belief that the Second Coming is imminent). He adjures his read-

* Compare the discussion of the Pastoral Epistles, above, pp. 134-136.

ers to eschew sensual things, seek the spiritual, maintain their faith, and keep themselves "in the love of God, looking for the mercy of our Lord Jesus Christ unto eternal life" (v. 21).

Historical and Literary Values. The letter is historically valuable for its characterization of the ways of the heretics, "ungodly men, turning the grace of our God into lasciviousness" (v. 4). Its literary value resides chiefly in (1) its colorful condemnations of the wicked: "clouds they are without water, carried about of winds; trees whose fruit withereth, without fruit, twice dead, plucked up by the roots; Raging waves of the sea, foaming out their own shame; wandering stars to whom is reserved the blackness of darkness for ever" (vss. 12-16); and (2) the beauty of its benedictory verses, which have been called "perhaps the noblest Doxology in Christian literature." [8]

Now unto him that is able to keep you from falling, and to present you faultless before the presence of his glory with exceeding joy, To the only wise God our Saviour, be glory and majesty, dominion and power, both now and ever. Amen.

THE SECOND EPISTLE OF PETER: A FINAL ADMONITION

This is probably the last-written book of the New Testament.

Authorship, Date, and Place. Although its first verse clearly states that its author was "Simon Peter, a servant and an apostle of Jesus Christ," virtually all commentators today agree that (1) the anonymous author attached the Apostle's name to it in order to lend it authority; (2) the author was not the author of I Peter; and (3) the letter is very "late," probably to be dated about A.D. 150. Some such date is indicated by the following facts: (1) It incorporates almost the whole of the Epistle of Jude in 2:2-17; most scholars agree that II Peter is the borrower. (2) It mentions (3:4) the death of "the fathers"—the early church leaders. (3) It alludes to the Pauline epistles as "scriptures" (3:15-16), a term applied during the Apostolic Age only to the books of the Old Testament. Its place of composition is uncertain (probably Rome); its addressees were Christians (probably Gentiles), "them that have obtained like precious faith with us" (1:1).

Purposes. The purposes of the letter are almost identical with those of Jude: (1) to combat the Gnostic and Antinomian teachings, (2) to encourage Christians to hold on to their faith, and (3) to reaffirm the Parousia.

Contents. The principal addition this letter makes to Jude is the expansion of the teaching about the Second Coming. The author assures his readers that, though this glorious event has been so long delayed that many people have lost hope, it still *will* take place. One must remember that "one day is with the Lord as a thousand years, and a thousand years as one day" (3:8) * and that the Lord, who always keeps his promises, is merely delaying the day of judgment so that all men "should come to repentance" (3:9). Then the heavens will pass away, the earth will be destroyed by fire, and a new Golden Age of righteousness will follow. Therefore, every man should live a holy life so as to remain in readiness.

Like Jude, the letter closes with a benedictory doxology.

* Compare Psalm 90:4.

11

The Revelation of John: An Apocalypse

Apocalyptic writing has sometimes been considered a type of prophecy, but it is actually a different literary genre. It is a preview of the end of the age and of the establishment of a new one. Usually appearing in eras of great oppression and persecution, it is nearly always filled with graphic and terrifying accounts of disasters which will put an end to the persecution. Because such predictions during times of persecution are always dangerous for the author, a secret sort of symbolism, a cryptic language, is usually employed—symbols and language which will be understood by the persecuted but not by the oppressors. Hence we find strange beasts, angels, mystical numbers, stars, vials, and such phrases as "son of man," "the ancient of days," "the locusts of torment," "a woman clothed with the sun," and so on. The use of this language and symbology explains why apocalyptic writing is so puzzling to many modern readers. It was *intended* to puzzle the uninitiated.

Revelation is not the only example of apocalyptic literature in the Bible. Isaiah 24–27, written during the Assyrian harassment in the seventh century B.C.; Ezekiel 37, written during the tribulations inflicted by the Babylonians in the sixth century B.C.; and the last six chapters of Daniel, written during the persecutions of Antiochus Epiphanes in the second century B.C.—all these are apocalyptic, as well as Zechariah 9–14, Joel 3, Mark 13, Matthew 24, Luke 21, I Corinthians 15, Jude, II Peter, II Thessalonians 1–2, and scattered passages in some of the other epistles.

AUTHORSHIP, DATE, AND PURPOSE

The Roman Catholic title for this last of the New Testament books is simply "The Apocalypse." In the King James Version it is

"The Revelation of St. John the Divine." * Although tradition holds that the John referred to is the Apostle John, virtually all liberal scholars disagree and think that the author was perhaps an elder in the church at Ephesus. For a while he appears to have been in exile on the island of Patmos, where, he tells us, he had the apocalyptic visions; but the actual writing was probably done later at Ephesus.

The occasion for the writing of Revelation was almost certainly the cruel treatment of Christians by the Emperor Domitian about A.D. 96. All the Roman emperors from Caesar Augustus on had been proclaimed divine; three of them—Caligula, Nero, and Domitian—took the ascription of divinity seriously and tried to enforce worship of themselves upon all their subjects. The Christians' refusal to comply exposed them to the most drastic punishment. The book of Revelation was written to encourage them to be faithful at all costs, even unto death, and to reassure them that the age of wickedness had now reached its culmination, would soon come to an end, and would be succeeded by a new age of freedom and happiness under the rule of Jesus himself.

Some commentators have considered the book a projection of the centuries-old longing of the Hebrews for freedom from persecution. It must be admitted that in it the Christian ethic of forgiveness of one's enemies is completely lacking. But Revelation is a thoroughly and distinctly *Christian* book, with the risen Christ as the central figure. Unlike the Messiah promised by the Old Testament prophets, Christ will not simply defeat the enemies of the faithful and establish a new kingdom; at his Second Coming he will entirely overturn the whole order of existence and create a new heaven and a new earth, over which God the Father and Jesus his Son will reign in righteousness forever.

The book is addressed to "the seven churches of Asia"—those at Ephesus, Smyrna, Pergamum, Thyatira, Sardis, Philadelphia, and Laodicea; and there is a specific message for each of those churches. It is generally agreed, however, that the principal messages of the book were intended for Christians everywhere.

---

* The word *divine* here means "theologian" or "preacher."

STYLE

The author borows copiously from the imagery and phraseology of the prophetic books of the Old Testament, especially Isaiah, Ezekiel, Zechariah, Daniel, Jeremiah, and Joel.[1] And the body of the book is built upon three conceptions derived from Jewish apocalyptic: (1) the coming of a Messiah, following a series of disasters; (2) the appearance of a demonic Antichrist as the enemy of the Messiah; and (3) the Messiah's establishment of a new world order.[2]

The book of Revelation has been of incalculable importance in the history of the Western world. To be sure, it has added little to Christian theological dogma, and it offers few moral precepts. It is true, too, that it has often been misunderstood and misinterpreted; sometimes it has led to fanaticism. But its stirring passages have brought consolation and hope to countless individuals throughout the Christian era.

Revelation is a superb piece of literature. The pictorial imagination of its author in unsurpassed even by that of Isaiah, Dante, or Blake. Its careful construction—shown especially in its three series of "woes," each followed by a brief passage of rejoicing—prove its author a master of architectonics. It never lags, but builds to a resounding climax in Chapters 12–14, and ends in a triumphant dénouement. Its ability to inspire other creators of literature and the arts is attested by such works as Dante's *Divine Comedy,* Milton's *Paradise Lost,* Bunyan's *Pilgrim's Progress,* Van Eyck's "Adoration of the Lamb," Michelangelo's "Last Judgment," Tintoretto's "Paradiso," and Holman Hunt's "Light of the World." It is not too enthusiastic to say that the book of Revelation is the imaginative masterpiece of the New Testament.

VISION OF CHRIST (CH. 1)

John sees a vision of Christ and hears him say—"I am he that liveth, and was dead; and, behold, I am alive for evermore" (1:18). He is clothed in a long garment and a golden girdle; his hair is as white as wool, his eyes like a flame, his feet like burnished brass, and his voice like the "sound of many waters." In his right hand he holds seven stars (symbols of the angels of the seven churches), and from his mouth issues a "sharp two-edged sword." He orders John to write an account of the vision "and the things which are, and the things which shall be hereafter."

LETTERS TO THE SEVEN CHURCHES (CHS. 2–3)

John is told to praise the churches at Smyrna, Pergamum, Thyatira, and Philadelphia for their loyalty and bravery in persecution; but Sardis and Laodicea are rebuked for their tepidity. Ephesus, though commended, is warned against a decline of zeal; Pergamum is taken to task for tolerating two heretical groups; and Thyatira for listening to the immoral teaching of a false prophetess.

GOD AND THE SEALED BOOK (CHS. 4–5)

Reminiscent of visions in Isaiah 6 and Ezekiel 1 is John's vision of God the Father, seated upon a throne in heaven. Around the throne are twenty-four elders, clothed in white and wearing golden crowns. Nearby are four strange beasts, "full of eyes before and behind" (perhaps representing signs of the zodiac).[3] In his hand God holds a secret-filled book, which nobody can open until Jesus the Lamb breaks the seals which keep it closed. (Perhaps the author intended the book to represent the writings of the Old Testament prophets, whose words were known but whose meanings were obscure until Jesus came to interpret them).[4] The elders, now having harps and golden vials full of odors, "which are the prayers of saints," fall down before Christ and proclaim him worthy to open the seals.

DISASTERS OF THE FIRST SIX SEALS AND THE JOYS OF THE RIGHTEOUS (CHS. 6–7)

Christ opens one seal at a time, each disclosing a different vision. The first four reveal horses of different colors, each with a rider (the famous "Four Horsemen of the Apocalypse"): (1) a white horse, representing foreign invasion (perhaps by the Parthians, for the rider holds a bow, and the Parthians were renowned for their archery); (2) a red horse, representing civil strife; (3) a black horse, representing famine; and (4) a pale horse, representing pestilence and death. The fifth seal discloses the souls of the martyrs crying out for judgment upon their persecutors. The opening of the sixth seal shows a general cataclysm— an earthquake, the sun becoming "black as sackcloth of hair," the moon turning into blood, and the stars falling. Terrified, all human beings try to hide, and they beg the mountains and the rocks to fall on them and hide them from the wrath of the Lamb— for "the great day of his wrath is come." The opening of the seventh seal is deferred, while four angels, standing on the four corners of the earth, hold back the winds from harming all the "servants of God," who have come through great tribulations and "have washed their robes, and made them white in the blood of the Lamb." They will be comforted:

> They shall hunger no more, neither thirst any more;
> Neither shall the sun light on them, nor any heat.
> For the Lamb which is in the midst of the throne shall feed them,
> And shall lead them unto living fountains of waters:
> And God shall wipe away all tears from their eyes. (7:16-17)

THE SEVENTH SEAL AND THE SEVEN TRUMPETS
(CHS. 8–11)

The breaking of the seventh seal reveals not another calamity, but a group of seven angelic trumpeters, six of whom in turn proclaim more disasters: a hail of fire; a fiery mountain; a falling star called wormwood; an eclipse of the sun, moon, and stars; a plague of locusts with the stings of scorpions; a vast host of destroying horsemen from beyond the Euphrates. Upon the blowing of the seventh trumpet, great voices from heaven announce that

> The kingdoms of this world are become the kingdoms of our Lord,
> And of his Christ; and he shall reign for ever and ever. (11:15)

THE ANTICHRIST AND GOD'S PROMISE (CHS. 12–14)

The apocalypse now reaches its climax. There appear in heaven a "woman clothed with the sun" [the Hebrew nation?] and her child [Christ?]. A terrible red dragon [Rome?] "having seven heads [the seven hills of Rome?] and ten horns, and seven crowns upon his head" attempts to devour the child, but the child is caught up into heaven, and the woman flees into the wilderness.*

Next comes the war in heaven between "that old serpent called

---

* Compare the Egyptian myth of Isis, Horus, and Typhon and the Greek myth of Leto, Apollo, and the Python (T. Henshaw, *New Testament Literature* [London, George Allen and Unwin, 1952, p. 408]).

the Devil, and Satan" and the forces of good, led by the archangel Michael; Satan and his fellow rebels are cast out onto the earth.* There Satan continues his war with the woman and her offspring "which keep the commandments of God, and have the testimony of Jesus Christ."

Another beast arises from the sea and is given great power by the serpent Satan. Many scholars believe that John identifies the Beast with the emperor Nero, for he says that its number is "six hundred three score and six" (666)—"the numerical value of the letters in 'Nero Caesar' when added together (13:18)." [5] If the composition date was near the end of the first century, Nero had committed suicide some thirty years earlier. But John may be reviving an old legend which held that Nero had not died but had escaped to the East (Parthia), whence he would return at the head of an avenging army. Thus the wicked emperor becomes the symbol of the earthly powers of evil, the Antichrist, in league with Satan himself.

Again a voice from heaven promises that the steadfast will be blessed.

THE SEVEN VIALS OF WRATH (CHS. 15–18)

A third series of woes is now foretold. Seven angels appear, holding vials (or bowls) filled with the wrath of God. As each empties his vial, a new plague comes upon the men who bear the mark of the Beast: a plague of sores; the sea turned into blood; the rivers and fountains turned into blood; scorching heat from the sun; darkness of the Beast's kingdom; and the drying of the river Euphrates. The powers of evil then gather at Armageddon for a final battle with the forces of God (16:16). At the emptying of the seventh vial, a voice from heaven cries out: "It is done!" Lightning, thunder, and an earthquake follow; islands and mountains disappear; and great hailstones fall upon men.

Next one of the angels shows John a vision of a woman (evidently Rome) clothed in scarlet, purple, and jewels. In her hand is a cup full of abominations and filth, and on her forehead is written: "Mystery, Babylon the Great, the Mother of Harlots and Abominations of the Earth." She is drunk with the blood of the

---

* This event, told in three verses (12:7-9), is the framework upon which Milton, in *Paradise Lost*, built his account of the war in heaven.

saints and the martyrs. Another angel envisages the city's destruction, and there is great rejoicing in heaven.

THE TWO JUDGMENTS (CHS. 19–20)

In accordance with some ancient Jewish apocalypses, John tells of *two* days of judgment. First, Christ appears as a great military leader, on a white horse. The powers of evil gather against him (presumably at Armageddon); the Beast (Antichrist) and the False Prophet (Satan?) are captured, bound, and thrown into a lake of fire and brimstone, and all their followers are slain. The Christian martyrs, who had not worshipped the Beast, are restored to life and taken to heaven to reign with Christ for a thousand years (the Millennium). This is the first Judgment.

At the end of the Millennium, Satan will be released to prey upon mankind again and to regroup his followers (somehow restored, and now called Gog and Magog) for a final battle. Then the innumerable wicked are consumed by fire from heaven. All the dead are resurrected and brought before God's throne. An account of their deeds is read from the Book of Life, and final judgment is passed on them. The wicked, along with Satan and the Beast, are thrown into the lake of fire.

THE NEW JERUSALEM (CHS. 21:1—22:17)

A wondrous new place is prepared for the righteous. A new heaven and a new earth replace the old, and a New Jerusalem descends from God, which will henceforth be God's dwelling place with men:

And I heard a great voice out of heaven saying, Behold, the tabernacle of God is with men, and he will dwell with them, and they shall be his people, and God himself shall be with them, and be their God. And God shall wipe away all tears from their eyes; and there shall be no more death, neither sorrow, nor crying, neither shall there be any more pain: for the former things are passed away. (21:3-4)

The walls of the city are like jasper; its foundations, of different precious stones; and its streets, of pure gold. God himself is its Temple and its source of light. The Tree of Life with twelve kinds of fruit provides food, and the River of Life flows through the city. "And let him that is athirst come. And whosoever will, let him take the water of life freely" (22:17).

CONCLUSION (22:18–21)

John concludes his book with a curse upon anybody who tampers with the words of his writings, a promise that Jesus will return soon, and a simple benediction: "The grace of our Lord Jesus Christ be with you all. Amen."

Notes*

NOTES TO CHAPTER 1: BACKGROUNDS OF
THE NEW TESTAMENT

[1] *DB* (*Dartmouth Bible*), p. 844.

[2] For these and many of the following remarks concerning Pharisees, Sadducees, Zealots, and Essenes, see *DB*, pp. 850-853 and Enslin, "New Testament Times: II. Palestine," *IB* (*Interpreter's Bible*), VII, 111-112.

[3] See *DB*, p. 853.

[4] Dinsmore, pp. 263 and 266.

[5] Henshaw, p. 152. The following discussion comparing the four Gospels (including the reasons for the differences) is derived largely from Henshaw.

[6] See Gilmour, *IB*, VIII, 110.

[7] Several good harmonies of these books have been compiled. One of the best is *A Harmony of the Synoptic Gospels* by Ernest D. Burton and Edgar J. Goodspeed.

[8] For thorough and detailed studies of this topic, see Scott, pp. 21-32, and Perry, "The Growth of the Gospels," *IB*, VII, 61-62.

[9] Perry, *IB*, VII, 62.

NOTES TO CHAPTER 2: THE GOSPEL
ACCORDING TO MARK: THE EARLIEST OF THE SYNOPTICS

[1] For detailed discussions of the authorship of the Gospel of Mark, see Dinsmore, p. 168; Goodspeed, pp. 138, 155-156; Grant, *IB*, VII, 630-637; Henshaw, pp. 92-97; Jenney, p. 125; Macarthur, p. 386; Parmelee, pp. 170-172; Scott, pp. 55-59; and Sprau, pp. 406-407.

[2] See Torrey; see also Grant, *IB*, VII, 631.

[3] Jenney, p. 125.

[4] See Grant, *IB*, VII, 633-634.

[5] Scott, p. 61.

[6] Henshaw, pp. 107-108.

[7] Henshaw, p. 108.

* See *Bibliography* for information about authors and works listed in this section.

[8] Dinsmore, p. 268.

[9] *DB*, p. 859.

[10] Parmelee, p. 175.

[11] Scott, p. 62.

[12] The passage in Mark (1:2b-3) is really a jumble of quotations from Is. 40:3, Ex. 23:20, and Mal. 3:1. See Grant, *IB*, VII, 648-649.

[13] *DB*, p. 965.

[14] Grant, *IB*, VII, 712.

[15] Grant, *IB*, VII, 742.

[16] Grant, *IB*, VII, 738.

[17] "Of Adversity."

[18] Title from *DB*, p. 938.

[19] According to Grant (*IB*, VII, 787-788) the three passages were originally one.

[20] Grant, *IB*, VII, 671. Grant points out that curing the paralytic did not prove that Jesus was the Messiah, for even the promised Messiah was not expected to grant forgiveness. The Jewish penalty for blasphemy was stoning.

[21] Luccock, *IB*, VII, 747.

[22] Grant, *IB*, VII, 761-762.

[23] Grant, *IB*, VII, 795-798.

[24] The phrase "den of thieves" does not necessarily imply that the money-changers and merchants were acting dishonestly. Jesus' main objection is that the Temple has become a bazaar full of noise and the smell of animals and the chaffering of merchants and buyers, whereas it should be a holy place. It is entirely possible—even likely —that the merchants and money-changers were making undue profits from their transactions, but Mark does not say so. See Grant, *IB*, VII, 828-830.

[25] Lake, p. 46.

[26] Grant, *IB*, VII, 851.

[27] Various reasons for Judas' treachery have been offered. See Grant, *IB*, VII, 871-872.

[28] Grant, *IB*, VII, 765.

[29] Grant, *IB*, VII, 767-768.

[30] *DB* (p. 972) suggests that the inclusion of Moses and Elijah in the Transfiguration is meant to imply that Jesus was an embodiment of the Law (represented by Moses) and of the prophets (represented by Elijah).

[31] Grant, *IB*, VII, 867. As Grant points out, the commemoration of the Exodus had been "long since combined with the immemorial springtime agricultural festival of *Maççôth. . . .*"

[32] For discussions of the illegality of this trial, see *DB*, p. 978, and Grant, *IB*, VII, 887.

[33] For various suggested solutions to the problems raised by the abrupt ending as found in v.8 and the addition of the epilogue, see Grant, *IB*, VII, 915-916, and Scott, pp. 59-60. Some scholars believe that the abruptness of the ending of v.8 is appropriate and in keeping with the abrupt opening of the Gospel. The most likely solution seems to be that the last page of the original manuscript was lost and that some editor supplied the epilogue to make clear that the prophecies of Jesus' reappearance to the Disciples in Galilee were fulfilled.

NOTES TO CHAPTER 3: THE GOSPEL ACCORDING TO MATTHEW: THE FULLEST ACCOUNT OF THE LIFE AND TEACHINGS OF JESUS

[1] Quoted (in French) by Sypherd, p. 164.

[2] P. 65.

[3] Scott, pp. 65-66. See also Sherman E. Johnson, *IB*, VII, 232.

[4] Eusebius is quoted by Johnson, *IB*, VII, 240.

[5] Parmelee, p. 180. Sypherd (p. 164) says that only five hundred verses in Matthew are derived from Mark.

[6] Summarized from Johnson, *IB*, VII, 236.

[7] Scott, p. 68.

[8] P. 164.

[9] Sypherd, p. 164.

[10] Henshaw, pp. 117-118.

[11] Macarthur, p. 372.

[12] Henshaw, p. 113.

[13] Scott, p. 67. Other commentators who nominate Antioch are *DB*, p. 859; Goodspeed, pp. 175-176; Parmelee, pp. 177-179; and Streeter (see Johnson, *IB*, VII, 241).

[14] Johnson, *IB*, VII, 241.

[15] *DB*, p. 859.

[16] *DB*, p. 859.

[17] Scott, pp. 67-68, and Johnson, *IB*, VII, 241.

[18] The eminent scholar Goodspeed (pp. 176-177) dates the book "about 80." Henshaw (pp. 113-114) suggests 80-90; Johnson (*IB*, VII, 241), "not far from the year 100"; Macarthur (p. 396), about 90; Parmelee (p. 182), 80-90; and Scott (pp. 67-68), 90-95.

[19] Henshaw, p. 113.

[20] *IB*, VII, 240.

[21] Goodspeed, p. 158.

[22] Henshaw, p. 123.

²³ Sprau, p. 407.

²⁴ Johnson, *IB*, VII, 235.

²⁵ Dinsmore, p. 267. Some of the other merits and faults mentioned here have been pointed out by Dinsmore; by *DB* (p. 869); by Henshaw (pp. 126-127); and by Sypherd (p. 165).

²⁶ Henshaw, pp. 123-124, and Johnson, *IB*, VII, 234.

²⁷ Charles H. Buck, Jr., cited by Johnson, *IB*, VII, 238, note 15.

²⁸ Scott, p. 68; Henshaw, p. 120; and Johnson, *IB*, VII, 238.

²⁹ Listed with Biblical references by Henshaw, p. 120.

³⁰ Johnson, *IB*, VII, 251.

³¹ For a discussion of the confused chronology of Herod's death and Jesus' birth, see *DB*, pp. 963-964.

³² *DB*, p. 972. For a brief summary of the debates, see *DB*, pp. 971-972.

³³ See Johnson, *IB*, VII, 514-515.

NOTES TO CHAPTER 4: THE GOSPEL ACCORDING TO LUKE: THE MOST POETIC AND ARTISTIC OF THE SYNOPTICS

¹ Quoted (in French) by Sypherd, p. 166.

² Chase, p. 269.

³ Marcion the Heretic (*ca.* A.D. 140), the author of the Muratorian Fragment (*ca.* 170), and Irenaeus (*ca.* 185) all ascribe the book to Luke. See Henshaw, p. 130; also *IB*, VIII, 3.

⁴ *DB*, p. 860; this same work says that most Roman Catholics and conservative Protestants date the Gospel *ca.* A.D. 70. Goodspeed (p. 196) and Macarthur (p. 396) agree on *ca.* A.D. 90. Henshaw (p. 137) suggests A.D. 75-85. See also Gilmour, *IB*, VIII, 9-10; and Scott, pp. 67-68 and 92-94.

⁵ See *DB*, p. 860; Henshaw, p. 136; and Scott, p. 67.

⁶ Gilmour, *IB*, VIII, 28.

⁷ Henshaw, pp. 134-135; also Scott, pp. 77-80.

⁸ Macarthur, p. 404.

⁹ Henshaw, pp. 139-142.

¹⁰ Gilmour, *IB*, VIII, 18. Sypherd (p. 165) estimates that 320 verses (27.8 per cent) of Luke comes from Mark. Scott (p. 83) estimates 40 per cent.

¹¹ Goodspeed, p. 205.

¹² Macarthur, p. 398. Goodspeed (p. 205) lists good reasons for the "Great Omission." Henshaw (p. 132) posits a faulty manuscript of Mark.

¹³ Gilmour, *IB*, VIII, 18-19.

¹⁴ Scott, pp. 82-83.

¹⁵ Scott, p. 83. Sypherd (p. 165) says 250 verses, or 21 per cent.

[16] Henshaw, p. 131, and Gilmour, *IB*, VIII, 14-15.

[17] Scott, p. 83. Sypherd (p. 165) says 850 verses, or about 51 per cent.

[18] Henshaw, pp. 131-133, and Scott, p. 84.

[19] These pieces of criticism are derived chiefly from Chase, pp. 269-276; Gilmour, *IB*, VIII, 3-4; Henshaw, pp. 135, 142-143; Macarthur, p. 399; Scott, p. 84; and Sypherd, pp. 166-167.

[20] Gilmour (*IB*, VIII, 34-35) points out that Luke is especially interested in punitive miracles (see Acts 1:18, 5:5, 10; 12:23; and 13:11).

[21] Gilmour, *IB*, VIII, 38.

[22] Some old Latin manuscripts attribute the Magnificat to Elisabeth. The song is similar to Hannah's hymn of praise in I Sam. 2:1-10; and the conception of Samuel is more closely parallel to that of John the Baptist than to that of Jesus (Gilmour, *IB*, VIII, 41-42).

[23] C.G. Montefiore, quoted by Gilmour, *IB*, VIII, 195.

[24] Gilmour (*IB*, VIII, 240-241) suggests (1) that the parable found in Luke may be the source of Mark's story of Christ's cursing the fig tree (Mark 11:12-14); and (2) that three (in "three years," Luke 13:7) is a "recurring number in folktales." Findlay (p. 1047) interprets the parable allegorically: the fig tree is Jerusalem, the vineyard is Palestine, and God is the owner who has so far spared Jerusalem despite its wickedness.

[25] Some commentators have regarded the passage not as a parable but as a set of rules for etiquette or as a series of proverbs. See Buttrick, *IB*, VIII, 252-253. Findlay (p. 1047) suggests that v.12 is a thrust at Jesus' host for excluding the poor, the maimed, the halt, and the blind from his list of guests.

[26] Gilmour, *IB*, VIII, 256.

[27] Gilmour, *IB*, VIII, 283.

[28] Edwin M. Poteat, paraphrased by Buttrick, *IB*, VIII, 283. For another interpretation, see Findlay, p. 1049.

[29] For these interpretations and others, see Buttrick and Gilmour, *IB*, VIII, 291-293. Gilmour (p. 289) cites an Egyptian story of the first century A.D. that is similar to the parable.

[30] See Gilmour, *IB*, VIII, 306-308.

[31] Henshaw, p. 139. The remainder of my paragraph is mainly a summary of this page from Henshaw.

[32] Gilmour, *IB*, VIII, 146.

[33] Gilmour, *IB*, VIII, 408.

[34] The King James Version, following some inferior manuscripts, states that Christ ate honeycomb as well as fish (Gilmour, *IB*, VIII, 432).

NOTES TO CHAPTER 5: THE ACTS OF THE APOSTLES: THE EARLIEST HISTORY OF THE SPREAD OF CHRISTIANITY

[1] For arguments both for and against Luke's authorship, see Henshaw, pp. 182-186, and Scott, pp. 88-92.

[2] For discussions of the sources of Acts, and especially of the "we" passages, see Goodspeed, pp. 197-209; Henshaw, pp. 193-194; and Scott, pp. 104-106.

[3] See Goodspeed, p. 196; Scott, pp. 92-94; and Sypherd, p. 167. Henshaw (pp. 188-189) suggests between 75 and 85; Macarthur (p. 428) gives "about 80."

[4] An unnamed commentator, quoted by Henshaw, p. 193.

[5] See Henshaw, p. 200, and Scott, p. 104. For discussions of the historical accuracy of Acts, from which these paragraphs are taken, see DB, pp. 973, 993-994; Henshaw, pp. 194-200; and Scott, pp. 102-104.

[6] Quoted by Sypherd, p. 168. Chase (pp. 185-186) calls special attention to Luke's portraits and dramatic episodes.

[7] Syllabus suggested by Jenney, pp. 135-136; Macarthur, pp. 430-431; Scott, pp. 98-99; and Sypherd, pp. 167-168.

[8] Macgregor, IB, IX, 41-43. This exegete calls the sermon "the first Christian apology," and directs attention to the "primitive Christology" of the sermon, which suggests that Luke was following a documentary source.

[9] DB, p. 1032.

[10] "Daily ministration" (6:1) may refer to material needs in general and not specifically to food, and "tables" (v.2) may then refer to money-changers' tables rather than dining tables, in which case the whole passage can be interpreted as dealing with financial matters as a whole and not merely the providing of food for the needy. For these interpretations and the suggestion that the seven deacons were specially appointed to be apostles for the Hellenist Christians (as opposed to the Judean ones), see Macgregor, IB, IX, 88-91.

[11] He claims that he is "some great one." See Macgregor, IB, IX, 109-111.

[12] Chase (see note 6, above), p. 286.

[13] DB, p. 1041, and Macarthur, p. 491.

[14] There is some doubt concerning the illegality of the mob's actions. DB (p. 1033) says that the stoning was "not mere mob fury but an ancient and communal form of execution after formal trial." But did the Sanhedrin, which apparently had to appeal to Pilate in order to secure the death penalty for Jesus, have the authority to turn Stephen over to the mob for stoning? See Macgregor, IB, IX, 93.

[15] Tertullian (*ca.* A.D. 160-230), *Apologeticus.*

[16] According to Josephus, cited by Macgregor, *IB*, IX, 146.

[17] See Macarthur, p. 420. The biographical facts in this sketch are derived from Macarthur, pp. 420-427, and from Hatch, *IB*, VII, 187-199.

[18] All these dates are drawn from Hatch, *passim*, except for the first three entries, which come from Macarthur, pp. 420-422. They do not agree in all cases with those given above by Barrois (see chart, p. 3).

[19] *DB*, p. 1032.

[20] See Macgregor, *IB*, IX, 167. In Acts 13:1 Luke mentions that there were "prophets and teachers" in the Church at Antioch, and it was the prophet Agabus who informed that Church that a great famine was imminent (Acts 11:28). For a discussion of the role of New Testament prophets, see Macgregor, pp. 152-153.

[21] See Macgregor, *IB*, IX, 168.

[22] The reasons for Mark's defection can only be guessed at. Perhaps he was reluctant to preach to Gentiles, or maybe he was resentful of Paul's superseding Barnabas as leader of the mission. See Macgregor, *IB*, IX, 174.

[23] This Antioch was really not in Pisidia but in Phrygia, near the Pisidian border. See Macgregor, *IB*, IX, 176.

[24] There is disagreement about the meaning of James' words "abstain from pollution of idols, and from fornication, and from things strangled, and from blood." See Macgregor, *IB*, IX, 203-204.

[25] Despite the decision of the Jerusalem council, the dispute seems to have continued for some time. See Paul's complaint in Gal. 2:1-16. There is some scholarly disagreement whether Peter and Barnabas sided with the "circumcision party" *before* or *after* the council in Jerusalem. See *DB*, p. 1036, and Macgregor, *IB*, IX, 195-200.

[26] In Gal. 2:11-13 Paul complains that Barnabas was "carried away" by the arguments of the "circumcision party." Disagreement on this point may have been the real reason for the break between Paul and Barnabas. See Macgregor, *IB*, IX, 209.

[27] See Macgregor, *IB*, IX, 211-212, 265-266.

[28] "Asia" here means either the Roman province of Asia, consisting of Mysia, Lydia, and Caria, or perhaps the cities of the Aegean coast and nearby regions. See Macgregor, *IB*, IX, 214.

[29] Macgregor, *IB*, IX, 238.

[30] Macgregor, *IB*, IX, 238.

[31] Acts 20:3 says only, "And there he [abode] three months." There is no doubt, however, that "there" means "at Corinth." See Macgregor, *IB*, IX, 264.

[32] *DB*, p. 1038.

[33] This quotation is only one example of the preservation (both oral and written) of sayings of Jesus which are not found in the canonical Scriptures. Some of these *logia* are preserved in the writings of the Fathers of the Church and on scattered fragments of papyrus. See *DB*, pp. 1038-1039.

[34] See Macgregor, *IB*, IX, 345. This commentator calls attention to a "charming archaism" in the King James Bible. In 28:13 the phrase "fetched a compass" means "made a circuit" (Revised Standard Version), not "obtained a magnetic needle."

NOTES TO CHAPTER 6: THE GOSPEL ACCORDING TO JOHN: THE MOST PHILOSOPHICAL GOSPEL

[1] See Macgregor, *IB*, IX, 351-352.

[2] Quoted in *DB*, p. 860.

[3] See Henshaw, pp. 148-151; also Scott, pp. 236-239 and 242-244; Howard, *IB*, VIII, 440-441; and Parmelee, p. 201.

[4] See Scott, pp. 234-235.

[5] See Goodspeed, pp. 314-315; Henshaw, p. 148; Howard, *IB*, VIII, 440; Macarthur, p. 409.

[6] See A. Powell Davies, p. 107 and *passim*.

[7] See Garvie, *ABC*, pp. 1062-1066; also Henshaw, pp. 151-152; Howard, *IB*, VIII, 438-442; Parmelee, pp. 202-211; and Scott, pp. 258-259.

[8] See Howard, *IB*, VIII, 441-442; Macarthur, p. 408; Scott, p. 235; and A. Powell Davies, p. 107.

[9] Howard, *IB*, VIII, 441.

[10] Howard, *IB*, VIII, 438-441.

[11] See Scott, p. 253; also Henshaw, pp. 174-176.

[12] See Scott, p. 253.

[13] See Henshaw, pp. 166-167.

[14] See Macarthur, p. 413; also Henshaw, p. 168, and Scott, p. 249.

[15] Watts, p. 412. A. Powell Davies (pp. 107-108) remarks that John's "priestly and liturgical" style is strikingly similar to that of some of the Essene material in the Dead Sea texts.

[16] *DB*, p. 1149.

[17] Henshaw, p. 157.

[18] Both quotations from Henshaw, p. 160.

[19] Henshaw, p. 156.

[20] B.W. Streeter, quoted by Henshaw, p. 179.

[21] *DB*, p. 1164, and Howard, *IB*, VIII, 463-464.

[22] Howard, *IB*, VIII, 493-494. This commentator calls attention to: (1) some rather remote parallels to Christ's miracles in legends about the Greek god Dionysus as reported in the works of Pausanias and

Pliny; and (2) two passages in Philo's works in which the Logos is represented as a dispenser of spiritual wine.

[23] Some commentators, puzzled by the Synoptic Gospels' failure to record this miracle, have interpreted it as an "allegorical development" of the Parable of the Rich Man and Lazarus, found in Luke 16:19-31. See Howard, *IB*, VIII, 649, and Garvie, *ABC*, pp. 1080-1081.

[24] See Howard, *IB*, VIII, 593.

[25] The King James Version uses the word *condemn*, but the Greek word means "to pass sentence" (Howard, *IB*, VIII, 593).

[26] Howard, *IB*, VIII, 624.

[27] Howard, *IB*, VIII, 717.

[28] Howard, *IB*, VIII, 660.

[29] Howard, *IB*, VIII, 695-696.

NOTES TO CHAPTER 7: THE EPISTLES OF PAUL

[1] Scott, p. 125.

[2] Scott, p. 128.

[3] *DB*, p. 1074.

[4] *OAB* (Oxford Annotated Bible), p. 1385.

[5] Scott, pp. 130 and 140.

[6] See Scott, p. 144.

[7] For a discussion of these problems, see Scott, pp. 146-148.

[8] *OAB*, p. 1408.

[9] See Beare, *IB*, XI, 134-137.

[10] See Barnett, pp. 91-92, and Knox, *IB*, XI, 556-557.

[11] Scott, p. 177.

[12] For a thorough discussion, see Beare, *IB*, X, 597-603.

[13] Scott, p. 181.

NOTES TO CHAPTER 8: THE EPISTLE TO THE HEBREWS

[1] Henshaw, 344.

[2] See Scott, p. 199, and Purdy, *IB*, XI, 593-594.

[3] Purdy, *IB*, XI, 593.

[4] Scott, p. 199. Long ago Professor Andrew Sledd of Emory University facetiously remarked that "The Epistle of Paul the Apostle to the Hebrews" was an excellent title except that the work was not an epistle; it was not written by Paul; Paul was not an Apostle; and it was not addressed to the Hebrews.

NOTES TO CHAPTER 9: THE PASTORAL EPISTLES

[1] For a thorough discussion of authorship, see Scott, pp. 193-194 and Henshaw, pp. 321-328.

[2] See Henshaw, pp. 332–334, and Scott, p. 194.

[3] Henshaw, p. 324.

[4] Scott, p. 193.

NOTES TO CHAPTER 10: THE GENERAL
(OR CATHOLIC) EPISTLES

[1] Scott, p. 217.

[2] Henshaw, pp. 351-359, and Scott, pp. 209-212.

[3] For details, see Henshaw, pp. 377-378, and Barnett, pp. 242-247.

[4] Summarized from Scott, pp. 263-264.

[5] See Barnett, pp. 263-264; Henshaw, pp. 389-390; and Scott, pp. 225-226.

[6] Barnett, p. 264.

[7] Barnett, p. 265.

[8] Henshaw, pp. 391-392.

NOTES TO CHAPTER 11: THE REVELATION OF JOHN:
AN APOCALYPSE

[1] For an interesting list of specific borrowings, see Henshaw, pp. 405-414.

[2] Scott, p. 278.

[3] *DB*, pp. 1187-1188.

[4] Henshaw, p. 406.

[5] Scott, p. 279.

Bibliography

The Abingdon Bible Commentary. Nashville, Tenn.: Abingdon Press, 1929. Articles and commentaries by a number of authorities.

Albright, William F. *From the Stone Age to Christianity*. Rev. ed. Baltimore, Md.: Johns Hopkins Press, 1957. Reprinted in paperback by Anchor Books (Doubleday).

Baly, Denis. *The Geography of the Bible*. New York: Harper & Brothers, 1957.

Barnett, Albert. *The New Testament: Its Making and Meaning*. Rev. ed. Nashville, Tenn.: Abingdon Press, 1958.

Barrois, George A. "Chronology, Metrology, etc.," *The Interpreter's Bible*. Nashville, Tenn.: Abingdon Press, 1952. I, 142-164.

Bartlett, J. Vernon. "The Life and Work of Paul," *Abingdon Bible Commentary*. Nashville, Tenn.: Abingdon Press, 1929. Pp. 931-943.

Bates, Ernest S., ed. *The Bible Designed To Be Read as Living Literature*. New York: Simon and Schuster, 1936.

Beare, Francis W. Introduction and Exegesis to Colossians, *The Interpreter's Bible*. Nashville, Tenn.: Abingdon Press, 1955. XI, 133-241.

Bowie, Walter R. *The Story of the Bible*. Nashville, Tenn.: Abingdon Press, 1934.

――――. "The Parables," *The Interpreter's Bible*. Nashville, Tenn.: Abingdon Press, 1951. VII, 165-175.

――――, John Knox, George A. Buttrick, and Paul Scherer. Exposition to Luke, *The Interpreter's Bible*. Nashville, Tenn.: Abingdon Press, 1952. VIII, 26-434.

Browne, Lewis. *The Graphic Bible*. New York: Macmillan Co., 1928.

Bruce, F. F. *The English Bible: A History of Translations from the Earliest English Versions to the New English Bible*. New York: Oxford University Press, 1961.

Burch, Ernest W. Commentary on Acts, *Abingdon Bible Commentary*. Nashville, Tenn.: Abingdon Press, 1929. Pp. 1094-1134.

Burton, Ernest D., and Edgar J. Goodspeed. *A Harmony of the Synoptic Gospels*. New York: Charles Scribner's Sons, 1917.

Butterworth, Charles C. *The Literary Lineage of the King James Bible, 1340-1611*. Philadelphia: University of Pennsylvania Press, 1941.

163

Buttrick, George A. Exposition to Matthew, *The Interpreter's Bible*. Nashville, Tenn.: Abingdon Press, 1951. VII, 250-625.

Chamberlin, Roy B., and Herman Feldman, eds. *The Dartmouth Bible*. 2nd ed. Boston: Houghton Mifflin Co., 1961. An abridgment of the King James Version, with introductions, prefaces, notes, and annotated maps.

Charles, R. H. *Religious Development between the Old and the New Testaments*. New York: Oxford University Press, 1914.

Chase, Mary Ellen. *The Bible and the Common Reader*. Rev. ed. New York: Macmillan Co., 1952. Reprinted in paperback.

Colwell, Ernest C. *The Study of the Bible*. Chicago: University of Chicago Press, 1937.

Davies, A. Powell. *The Meaning of the Dead Sea Scrolls*. New York: New American Library, 1956.

Davies, J. Newton. Commentary on Mark, *Abingdon Bible Commentary*. Nashville, Tenn.: Abingdon Press, 1929. Pp. 996-1021.

————, Commentary on Matthew, *Abingdon Bible Commentary*. Nashville, Tenn.: Abingdon Press, 1929. Pp. 953-995.

Dibelius, Martin. *From Tradition to Gospel*. Translated by B. L. Woolf. New York: Charles Scribner's Sons, 1935.

Dinsmore, Charles Allen. *The English Bible as Literature*. Boston: Houghton Mifflin Co., 1931.

Elmslie, W. A. L. Introduction and Exegesis to I and II Chronicles, *The Interpreter's Bible*. Nashville, Tenn.: Abingdon Press, 1951. III, 341-548.

Enslin, Morton S. "New Testament Times: II. Palestine," *The Interpreter's Bible*. Nashville, Tenn.: Abingdon Press, 1951. VII, 100-113.

Farmer, W. R. *Maccabees, Zealots, and Josephus: An Inquiry into Jewish Nationalism*. New York: Columbia University Press, 1956.

Ferris, Theodore P. Exposition to Acts, *The Interpreter's Bible*. Nashville, Tenn.: Abingdon Press, 1954. IX, 24-349.

Findlay, J. A. Commentary on Luke, *Abingdon Bible Commentary*. Nashville, Tenn.: Abingdon Press, 1929. Pp. 1022-1059.

Gardiner, J. H. *The Bible as English Literature*. New York: Charles Scribner's Sons, 1927.

Garvie, Alfred E. Commentary on John, *Abingdon Bible Commentary*. Nashville, Tenn.: Abingdon Press, 1929. Pp. 1060-1093.

Gilmour, S. MacLean. Introduction and Exegesis to Luke, *The Interpreter's Bible*. Nashville, Tenn.: Abingdon Press, 1952. VIII, 3-434.

Goodspeed, Edgar J. *An Introduction to the New Testament*. Chicago: University of Chicago Press, 1937.

Gossip, Arthur J. Exposition to John, *The Interpreter's Bible*. Nashville, Tenn.: Abingdon Press, 1952. VIII, 463-811.

Grant, Frederick C. Introduction and Exegesis to Mark, *The Interpreter's Bible*. Nashville, Tenn.: Abingdon Press, 1951. VII, 629-917.

Guignebert, Charles. *The Jewish World in the Time of Christ*. Translated by S. H. Hooke, New York: E. P. Dutton & Co., 1939.

Harrison, R. K. *The Dead Sea Scrolls: An Introduction*. New York: Harper & Brothers, 1961.

Hatch, William H. P. "The Life of Paul," *The Interpreter's Bible*. Nashville, Tenn.: Abingdon Press, 1951. VII, 187–199.

Henshaw, T. *New Testament Literature*. London: George Allen and Unwin, 1952.

Howard, Wilbert F. Introduction and Exegesis to John, *The Interpreter's Bible*. Nashville, Tenn.: Abingdon Press, 1952. VIII, 437-811.

The Interpreter's Bible. 12 vols. Nashville, Tenn.: Abingdon Press, 1951-1957. The King James Version and the Revised Standard Version, side by side, with an introduction, interpretation, and notes for each book of the Bible, general articles, and outline maps. 148 editors, consulting editors, and contributors, representing a cross section of Protestant scholarship.

The Interpreter's Dictionary of the Bible. Edited by George A. Buttrick. 4 vols. Nashville, Tenn.: Abingdon Press, 1962. Entries for Biblical persons, places, objects, terms, and doctrines. Maps and illustrations.

Jenney, Ray F. *Bible Primer*. New York: Harper & Brothers, 1955.

Johnson, Sherman E. Introduction and Exegesis to Matthew, *The Interpreter's Bible*. Nashville, Tenn.: Abingdon Press, 1951. VII, 231-625.

Knox, John. Introduction and Exegesis to Philemon, *The Interpreter's Bible*. Nashville, Tenn.: Abingdon Press, 1955. XI, 555-573.

Lake, Kirsopp. *The Stewardship of Faith*. New York: G. P. Putnam's Sons, 1915.

Landis, Benson Y. *An Outline of the Bible, Book by Book*. New York: Barnes & Noble, Inc., 1963.

Luccock, Halford E. Exposition to Mark, *The Interpreter's Bible*. Nashville, Tenn.: Abingdon Press, 1951. VII, 647-917.

Macarthur, John R. *Biblical Literature and Its Backgrounds*. New York: Appleton-Century-Crofts, 1936.

Macgregor, G. H. C. Introduction and Exegesis to Acts, *The Interpreter's Bible*. Nashville, Tenn.: Abingdon Press, 1954. IX, 3-352.

May, Herbert G., and Bruce M. Metzger, eds. *The Oxford Annotated Bible*. New York: Oxford University Press, 1962. The Revised Standard Version, with introductions, notes, general articles, and maps.

Metzger, Bruce M. *An Introduction to the Apocrypha.* New York: Oxford University Press, 1957.

Miller, Madelaine S., and J. Lane. *Harper's Bible Dictionary.* 6th ed. New York: Harper & Brothers, 1959.

New Analytical Indexed Bible. Chicago: John A. Dickson Co., 1931.

Parmelee, Alice. *A Guidebook to the Bible.* New York: Harper & Brothers, 1948.

Perry, Alfred M. "The Growth of the Gospels," *The Interpreter's Bible.* Nashville, Tenn.: Abingdon Press, 1951. VII, 60-74.

Purdy, Alexander C. Introduction and Exegesis to Hebrews, *The Interpreter's Bible.* Nashville, Tenn.: Abingdon Press, 1955. XI, 577-763.

Robinson, Theodore H. "The History of Israel," *The Interpreter's Bible.* Nashville, Tenn.: Abingdon Press, 1952. I, 272-291.

Scott, Ernest F. *The Literature of the New Testament.* New York: Columbia University Press, 1936.

Sprau, George. *Literature in the Bible.* New York: Macmillan Co., 1932.

Sypherd, Wilbur O. *The Literature of the English Bible.* New York: Oxford University Press, 1938.

Taylor, Vincent. "The Life and Ministry of Jesus," *The Interpreter's Bible.* Nashville, Tenn.: Abingdon Press, 1951. VII, 114-144.

Torrey, Charles C. *Our Translated Gospels.* New York: Harper & Brothers, 1936.

Watts, Harold H. *The Modern Reader's Guide to the Bible.* Rev. ed. New York: Harper & Brothers, 1959.

Westminster Dictionary of the Bible. Rev. ed. Philadelphia: Westminster Press, 1944.

Index

(Page numbers in **boldface** indicate the principal treatment of a subject.)